T0135725

Markus Helfert
Howard Duncan (eds.)

# Cases and Projects
# in Business Informatics

## International
## Business Informatics Challenge and
## Conference 2008

Bibliografische Information der Deutschen Nationalbibliothek

Die Deutsche Nationalbibliothek verzeichnet diese Publikation in der
Deutschen Nationalbibliografie; detaillierte bibliografische Daten sind
im Internet über http://dnb.d-nb.de abrufbar.

ISBN 978-3-8325-2366-4

Logos Verlag Berlin GmbH
Comeniushof, Gubener Str. 47,
10243 Berlin
Tel.: +49 (0)30 42 85 10 90
Fax: +49 (0)30 42 85 10 92
INTERNET: http://www.logos-verlag.de

# Preface

Dublin City University (Ireland) hosted the Second International Business Informatics Challenge and Conference 2008. The aim of this international event is to exchange experience and findings between students and researchers and to encourage research in the field of Business Informatics and Information Systems. We invited bachelor and master students to submit projects and real-life case studies illustrating how technological solutions were developed and applied for effective information systems to solve the business needs of organisations. The papers presented in these proceedings show a wide range of technological innovations and applications of information and communications technology (ICT) and demonstrate solutions and challenges of ICT as a central element for organisations in the networked and multicultural economy of the 21st century.

All papers submitted to the International Business Informatics Challenge and Conference were reviewed by an international committee. This year the **PricewaterhouseCoopers Best Paper Award** was shared between Florian Moser from the University of Augsburg for his work "Project and Quality Management in a Student Software Development Project" and Mark Isenbarger, Jeff Davis and Brad Mier from Ball State University (USA). For "Automated Market Research: Capitalizing on the Foreseen Changes in the Market".

We would like to thank all those involved in contributing to the success of the International Business Informatics Challenge and Conference; without their enthusiastic support this competition and event would not be possible. A special thanks to our distinguished keynote speaker Prof. Fred L. Kitchens from Ball State University, U.S.A. We also would like to thank the authors and in particular the participants of the Business Informatics Challenge for their papers and personal contributions. We are especially grateful to the members of the programme committee and the supervisors for their reviews and valuable feedback to the authors. Without their commitment and time the review process would not be possible.

In addition, our thanks go to all our sponsoring and supporting organisations, in particular PricewaterhouseCoopers for sponsoring the best paper award. Finally, we thank Mr. Mouzhi Ge for his assistance in organising this event. We are

IV

looking forward to our next International Business Informatics Challenge and Conference in September 2008.

Dublin City University                                    Markus Helfert
August 2009                                               Howard Duncan

# Organisation of the Business Informatics Challenge

## Programme Committee and Supervisors

| | |
|---|---|
| Nadia Amin | U.K. |
| Saïd Assar | France |
| Gunnar Auth | Germany |
| Ulrike Baumöl | Germany |
| Malcolm Brady | Ireland |
| Cinzia Cappiello | Italy |
| Rommert J. Casimir | Netherlands |
| Mark W. S. Churn | U.S.A. |
| Dragan Cisic | Croatia |
| Regina Connolly | Ireland |
| Susana de Juana | Spain |
| Retha de la Harpe | South Africa |
| Jens Dibbern | Germany |
| Thang Le Dinh | Canada |
| Brian Donnellan | Ireland |
| Petr Doucek | Czech Republic |
| Joaquim Filipe | Portugal |
| Hans-Georg Fill | Austria |
| Melike Nur Findikoglu | U.S.A. |
| Owen Foley | Ireland |
| Andreas Gadatsch | Germany |
| Irit Askira Gelman | U.S.A. |
| Gy Hashim | Malaysia |
| Kevin Heffernan | Ireland |
| Armin Heinzel | Germany |
| Knut Hinkelmann | Switzerland |
| Jochen Hipp | Germany |
| Slinger Jansen | Netherlands |
| Reinhard Jung | Germany |
| Parwaiz Karamat | New Zealand |
| Karlheinz Kautz | Denmark |
| Abdelaziz Khadraoui | Switzerland |
| Fred L. Kitchens | U.S.A. |
| Barbara Klein | U.S.A. |
| Andy Koronios | Australia |
| Michael Lang | Ireland |
| Susanne Leist | Germany |
| Shuhua Liu | Finnland |
| Ewa Losiewicz-Dniestrzanska | Poland |
| Jin Nie | China |
| Rory O'Connor | Ireland |
| Mieczyslaw Lech Owoc | Poland |
| Susanne Patig | Germany |
| Daniel C. Phelps | U.S.A. |
| Ho Bao Quoc | Vietnam |

| | |
|---|---|
| Wolfgang Renninger | Germany |
| Mary Ann Robbert | U.S.A. |
| Paulo Rupino | Portugal |
| Petra Schmidt | Germany |
| Mohamad M. Sepehri | Iran |
| Vladimir Shekhovtsov | Ukraine |
| Marcin Sikorski | Poland |
| Simeon J. Simoff | Australia |
| Anongnart Srivihok | Thailand |
| William J. Tastle | U.S.A. |
| Georgi Todorov | Bulgaria |
| Margarita Todorova | Bulgaria |
| Inge van de Weerd | Netherlands |
| Johan Versendaal | Netherlands |
| Hao Wang | China |
| Fridolin Wild | Austria |
| Stanislaw Wrycza | Poland |
| Gregor Zellner | Germany |
| Lixuan Grace Zhang | U.S.A. |

## Programme Chairs and Organisers

Markus Helfert (Conference Chair)
Howard Duncan

School of Computing
Dublin City University, Ireland
{Markus.Helfert | Howard.Duncan} @computing.dcu.ie

## Associated Programme Chairs

Stanislaw Wrycza, University of Gdansk, Poland
Thang Le Dinh, Université de Moncton, Canada
Joaquim Filipe, Escola Superior de Tecnologia de Setúbal, Portugal

# International Business Informatics Challenge and Conference
## Thursday, 25th September 2008
## Dublin City University
## School of Computing
## Venue: Dublin City University - Invent Centre

| | |
|---|---|
| 9:15 – 9:20 | Registration |
| 9:20 – 9:30 | **Welcome and Opening Session**<br>*Markus Helfert, Howard Duncan* |
| 9:30 – 10:00 | **Keynote Presentation**<br>**The Challenges presented by Human Digital Memories**<br>*Cathal Gurrin*<br>*Dublin City University, Ireland* |
| 10:00 – 11:00 | **IT Risk Management at Supido**<br>*Lorenz Hartmann, Boris Toma, Christopher Zygor*<br>*University of Mannheim, Germany* |
| | **Automated Market Research: Capitalizing on the foreseen Changes in the Market**<br>*Jeff Davis, Mark Isenbarger, Brad Mier*<br>*Ball State University, U.S.A.* |
| 11:00 – 11:15 | **Coffee Break** |
| 11:15 – 12:45 | **Media Production and Editing: Capitalizing on the Foreseen Changes in the Market**<br>*Nicole Smith*<br>*Ball State University, U.S.A.* |
| | **A study of XP & Scrum: A Project Management Perspective**<br>*Michael Rooney, Frank Treacy, Sarah Slattery, Christina Staunton*<br>*National University of Ireland, Galway, Ireland* |
| | **Towards Optimized Manufacturing Scheduling**<br>*Jing Chyuan Tan*<br>*University of Bradford, UK* |
| 12:45 – 14:00 | **Lunch Break** |

| | |
|---|---|
| **14:00-15:00** | **Project Management – Software Development for Job Administration in a University Faculty**<br>*Florian Moser*<br>*University of Augsburg, Germany*<br><br>**An Algorithm of Data Fusion**<br>*Lei Qiu; Xiangan Heng; Hao Wang*<br>*National University of Defense Technology, Changsha, P.R.China,* |
| **15:00-15:15** | **Coffee Break**<br><br>**The PRICEWATERHOUSECOOPERS**<br>**Best Paper Award**<br><br>**Worth 500 Euro**<br><br>***PRICEWATERHOUSECOOPERS*** |
| **15:15-16:15** | **Discussion on Engaging Students and Supervising Student Project**<br><br>**Teaching Technology Through Immersive Projects: Tricks of the Trade**<br>*Fred L. Kitchens*<br>*Ball State University, U.S.A.*<br><br>**Experiences in engaging undergraduate students**<br>*Ray Walshe, Howard Duncan, Markus Helfert*<br>*Dublin City University, Ireland* |
| **16:15** | **Closing of Workshop** |

# TABLE OF CONTENTS

# A STUDY OF XP & SCRUM: A PROJECT MANAGEMENT PERSPECTIVE

Frank Treacy, f.treacy1@nuigalway.ie

Michael Rooney, m.rooney2@nuigalway.ie

Sarah Slattery, s.slattery2@nuigalway.ie

Christiana Staunton, c.staunton1@nuigalway.ie

Orla McHugh, orla.mchugh@nuigalway.ie

Business Information Systems Group, Department of Accountancy & Finance,

National University of Ireland, Galway.

## ABSTRACT

*This research examines agile software development from a project manager's perspective. It specifically investigates four different areas namely: project planning and scheduling; team selection; communication; and documentation on projects that use either Extreme Programming(XP) or Scrum as their software development methodology. Three organisations in Ireland participated in this study and one project manager from each organisation was interviewed. The size of the organisations, the level of experience of the project managers and the agile methodology in use varied across the organisation. The findings show that all project managers tended to be sceptical before implementing agile methodologies. However, post implementation they found that agile methodologies helped to improve their software development processes; provided the customer with a greater opportunity to work with the project team and also improved communication and collaboration amongst the project team. These elements contribute to a project team completing a more successful software development project.*

*Keywords: Agile methodologies, Project management, XP, Scrum*

## INTRODUCTION

In today's world companies are demanding information systems that constantly meet their changing requirements (Duane et al., 1999, pg 13). The traditional plan-driven software development methodologies are not able to cope with these changing requirements and they lack the flexibility and fast pace development to meet customers needs (Sridhar et al., 2005). Statistically, traditional projects have failed as can be seen in Figure 1 below (The Standish Group, 1995). Factors influencing these project failures included lack of user involvement, proper planning, smaller project milestones, competent staff and a clear vision and objectives.

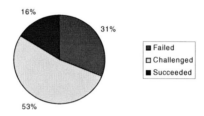

*Figure 1: Chaos Report Findings (The Standish Group, 1995)*

This has led to the development of an agile approach to software development, which also requires, project managers to adapt in order to successfully manage agile software development projects.

Project management of an agile software development project differs from that of a traditional software development project in several ways, which includes:

- Focusing on planning and scheduling using iterations as opposed to the traditional approach of planning and scheduling an entire project.
- Using teams that are smaller than traditional teams where team members are selected based on the skills required for the project.
- Including customers throughout the project and meeting on a daily basis for a short period of time in contrast to weekly meetings that are conducted on a traditional software development project (Cohn and Ford, 2003).
- Creating less but more useful documentation in comparison to traditional projects where large amounts of documentation can be created (Williams et al., 2003).

This project wishes to study the experiences of project managers that manage agile software development projects and how they handle project planning and scheduling; team selection; communication; and documentation which are the foundations of the Agile Manifesto as can be seen in section two below.

## AGILE SOFTWARE DEVELOPMENT

Agile software development came about in 2001 when seventeen prominent figures from the software development industry came together in Utah, United States of America, to discuss ways of creating software in a lighter, faster, more people-centric way. The outcome of the meeting was the creation of the Agile Manifesto, widely regarded as the definition of agile development. The Agile Manifesto (2001) favours:

> "***Individuals and interactions*** *over processes and tools*
>
> ***Working software*** *over comprehensive documentation*
>
> ***Customer collaboration*** *over contract negotiation*
>
> ***Responding to change*** *over following a plan"*

While the Agile Manifesto acknowledges there is value in the items on the right, it places more emphasis on the items on the left" (Agile Manifesto, 2001).

The Agile Manifesto (2001) also set down twelve principles for the agile software development. These are to:

- Satisfy the customer by providing quality software on time.
- Allow changes to the project requirements at any stage of the project.
- Produce software more often by reducing software lifecycles.
- Have business people and developers working together on a daily basis for the duration of the project.
- Create an environment where people are motivated, supported and trusted.
- Have face to face communication throughout the project.
- Use working software as the primary measure of progress.
- Make sure all stakeholders are working at a similar pace so that everyone knows what each person is working on.
- Pay attention to detail leading to a quality product.

- Keep things simple and focus on the work that needs to be done.
- Have self-organised teams.
- Monitor the project team's progress and review how it can improve.

There are several different agile methodologies in existence for software development. Each agile methodology follows the principles defined above. However, the focus of this project is on two of the most popular agile methodologies, namely Scrum and Extreme Programming(XP) (Fitzgerald et al., 2006). A brief introduction to both of these agile methodologies is detailed below.

**Extreme Programming (XP)** was designed to deliver software that focuses on customer needs and customer satisfaction (Highsmith, 2002, pg 67 - 69). It is based on the premise that software projects should be dynamic, in that you should be able to adapt to changing requirements at any point during the project lifecycle. This means that it is a more realistic and a better approach to software development than attempting to define all the requirements at the beginning of a project as is done using traditional software methods. XP uses face to face communication in place of written documentation wherever possible and attempts to achieve customer satisfaction through iterations which are followed by user-testing and acceptance. There is sometimes written documentation for the software, yet according to Jefferies (2001, pg 1 - 8) code is rarely or never documented.

**Scrum** provides flexibility in the development process and the ability to respond to change where factors such as requirements, resources and technology can be unpredictable and complex resulting in the delivery of a useful system (Schwaber, 1995). It allows for changing requirements throughout the project which are completed using a series of short iterations or sprints. A Sprint may last from one week to one month and there may be three to eight Sprints in one systems development process before the system is ready for distribution. Schwaber and Beedle (2002, pg 36) suggest that a Scrum team should comprise of between five and nine people. A study at AG Communication Systems by Rising et al (2000) agrees with this and state a team should have no more than ten people. If more than ten people are available then multiple teams should be formed.

Schwaber and Beedle (2002, pg 2) and Fitzgerald et al (2006) state that XP and Scrum complement each other well, with XP providing support for technical aspects and Scrum providing support for project planning and tracking. Research by Fitzgerald et al. (2006) also shows that Scrum and XP can be tailored and customised to suit the needs of different projects as they learned from their research at Intel, Shannon.

## Project Planning and Scheduling

In Scrum and XP, the underlying strategy of the selected agile methodologies is that of incremental development using a short development cycle (Leffingwell and Muirhead, 2004). This is evident in Scrum using the 30 day Sprint Cycle and in XP where a new release is made, often anywhere from daily to monthly.

Agile teams use three different levels of planning: release planning, iteration planning and daily planning (Cohn, 2006, pg. 28).

**Release planning** occurs at the start of a project to determine the scope, schedule and resources for each release. It is a very high level plan that covers the entire project. The project is broken into requirements known as user stories. Each user story is given story points or ideal days which reflect the size of the requirement. Ideal days is the estimated number of days to complete the user story whereas, story points are derived from a closed scale, for example, numbers 1 to 10, where 1 is the smallest user story and 10 is the largest user-story. For example, if it is known the team complete 40 story points for a fifteen day iteration, and the entire project is made up of 200 story points, it can be estimated that the project will require five iterations which is seventy five days.

An **iteration plan** is created in an iteration planning meeting. An iteration length is set and user stories from the release plan are prioritised to be developed within the iteration. Iterations can be timeboxed, which is the practise of fixing the iteration end date and not allowing it to change (Larman, 2004, pg 13). Iteration timeboxing is most commonly used in projects that require a large number of features that must be completed in a short space of time (Jalote et al.,

2004). The amount of work which can be completed within each iteration is estimated based on the same approach as above, where the known or estimated velocity of the team per iteration is used. The velocity of the team per iteration is the number of days it takes them to complete one iteration. The team takes a closer look at each user story and details a list of tasks that will have to be undertaken to implement each user story. Estimates are carried out on each task, primarily by the person who is going to implement the task with the aid of relevant parties. Unlike release planning, estimates in iteration planning are based on time (in hours) as shown in Table 1 below. Iterations provide key stakeholders with visibility to the product throughout the development process, which encourages feedback and allows for more successful product development (Larman, 2004).

|                   | Release Plan                | Iteration Plan |
|-------------------|-----------------------------|----------------|
| Planning Horizon  | 3-9 months                  | 1-4 weeks      |
| Items in Plan     | User Stories                | Tasks          |
| Estimated in      | Story Points or ideal days  | Ideal hours    |

*Table 1: Primary Differences between a Release and an Iteration Plan.*

Finally, there is **daily planning**. Most agile teams use some sort of daily stand-up meeting to coordinate work and synchronise daily efforts as can be seen in the daily scrum meeting. This daily planning is largely an informal process but teams make, assess, and review their plans during these meetings. In this meeting the team discuss what has been done since the last daily meeting and what will be done before the next daily meeting.

## Team selection for a project

Project teams are made up of several roles, for example: stakeholders, business analysts, designers, a project manager, programmers and testers. Individuals within the team have a variety of differing personalities, skills, ability, knowledge and temperament. Therefore, it is important to choose people who are team players and who have good people skills, so they will work together to build on each others strengths and accomplishments (Cockburn, 2001, pg 60, pg 169).

The size of an agile project team can depend on the number of requirements and how large the project is. With larger teams of more than ten people it is harder for each member of the team to know what other members of the team are working on and this can sometimes result in the duplication of work. The main emphasis behind smaller teams is that they are easier to manage and easier to control. Hence, for larger teams there is a greater need for more efficient communication and co-ordination (Cockburn, 2001, pg 126 -136, Sanjiv et al., 2005).

During a project, requirements can change and new pieces of functionality can be added. This may result in the project becoming larger, which can require extra team members. Cockburn (2001, pg 126 - 127) states that as the size of an agile project increases, the cost of communication increases, face to face communication can be more difficult to arrange, the quality of communication can sometimes decrease and software may become more difficult to develop. Therefore, there is a major need for control of agile development and team selection. This is done in order to monitor peoples work so that work is not duplicated to ensure an agile project is under control (Cockburn, 2001, pg 126 - 127).

## Communication

Communication is a dynamic process that individuals use to exchange ideas, experiences, and information through speaking, writing and body language. Good communication is at the core of successful projects. Open communication between team members and the project manager helps to make sure that project members are aware of potential risks and setbacks. Research shows that successful projects had project managers with good communication skills in contrast to failed projects which had project managers with poor communication skills (Ambler, 2002, pg 163 - 164, Sanjiv et al., 2005, The Standish Group, 1995). According to Ambler (2002, pg 159) communication is key to success on agile projects and is also one of the most crucial elements of both Extreme Programming (XP) and Scrum. In order for agile projects to succeed, the project team must create a highly communicative environment within which to work, as not doing this could increase the risk of failure (Ambler, 2002, pg 159 - 160).

Ambler (2002, pg 160 - 161) identifies several factors that affect communication within agile projects. These include:

- Physical proximity: the closer people are to one another then the greater the opportunities for communication.
- Temporal proximity: whether or not two people are working at the same time affects communication. Some people may be separated from co-workers by different time zones or by different working hours or schedules.
- Team Morale: the greater this is between the members of a team, then the greater the amount and quality of the information that is communicated.
- Tools: complicated software tools tend to act as barriers to communication.
- Anxiety about certain types of communication: Some people may prefer to speak on the phone or face to face, while others may avoid this type of communication and prefer e-mail. A method of communication that everyone is at ease with, and that will suit everyone for the duration of the project should be selected to overcome this anxiety.

Ambler (2002, pg 161 - 163) also identifies various different modes of communication for people to choose from when working together. These include: face to face at a white-board; face to face through having a conversation; video conversation; phone conversation; videotape; e-mail; audio-tape and paper. The most effective communication is face-to-face, especially through the use of white-boards as can be seen in Figure 2 below (Ambler, 2002, pg. 162).

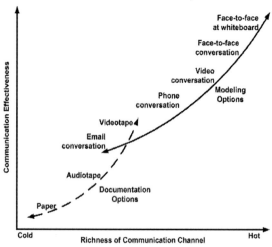

*Figure 2: Communication Effectiveness (Ambler, 2002, pg. 162)*

In summary, effective communication is an enabler of agile software development. It is critical that project teams are aware of all the different modes of communication available to them and they should pick the most suitable communication mode for their current situation. If a project is to succeed, the team must create a highly communicative environment and actively remove barriers to communication when they arise (Ambler, 2002, pg 164, Crushman, 1999, Sanjiv et al., 2005)

## Documentation

Documentation can be seen as a form of communication between the various parties involved in a project. According to Ambler (2002, pg 241 - 242) a document is anything whose purpose is to convey information in a persistent manner. In a traditional project there is less communication so there is a much greater need for documentation. In agile projects the team relies on informal internal communication so the need for documentation decreases (Hass, 2007). Figure 3 displayed below compares the agile approach and the traditional approach to the generation of documentation (Ambler, 2002).

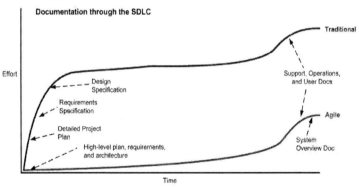

*Figure 3: Difference between agile and traditional documentation (Ambler, 2002)*

The agile approach is to delay the creation of all documents until as late as possible, creating them just before they are needed. By waiting to document information once it has stabilised it is possible to reduce both the cost and the risk associated with documentation. This does not mean that all documentation should be left towards the end (Ambler, 2002, pg 243). Notes should still be taken throughout development so that critical information is not lost or forgotten (Ambler, 2002, pg 244, Cockburn, 2001). There are also other reasons as to why documentation should be created for agile projects. These include:

- To support communication with an external group: it is not always possible to co-locate a development team or to have project stakeholders available at all times.
- To think something through: writing ideas down on paper can help to solidify them and helps people identify where potential problems may occur.

Agile developers recognise that it can be difficult to have just enough documentation, at the right time, for the right audience. A project team should concentrate on creating documentation that provides maximum value to its customers. An agile document just needs to be good enough for its intended audience. Although agile software development produces working software over comprehensive documentation that does not mean that documentation should not be created nor neglected (Ambler, 2002, pg 254, Cockburn, 2001).

## RESEARCH APPROACH

Case study was the research strategy adopted for this project. Multiple case studies were conducted in order to obtain a broader view of practices in several organisations and also to allow for comparison and analysis across different organisations. Additional cases studies would have been conducted if more time was available for the project. Other research approaches such as a survey method may have been used, but due to the limited timescales for this research project it may have been difficult to obtain access to the number of organisations required for quantitative analysis.

### Selection of Organisations

The main criteria used for the selection of organisations was to identify project managers working in organisations based in Galway (due to their proximity to the university) who were currently managing an agile project using either XP or Scrum. The team contacted a large number of companies based in Galway to determine if they were using agile methodologies. Three project managers were identified that were willing to participate in the research. Each of these project managers were working on teams that used XP or Scrum as their methodology for developing software.

## Data Collection

As the project team wished to gather detailed opinions and perspectives from each project manager semi-structured interviews were used to collect data. A number of open-ended and closed questions relating to each section detailed above were developed. The open-ended questions gave project managers the opportunity to state their opinion. The team ensured that the questions asked were not leading or biased. On completion of all the interviews the findings from each company were analysed and compared. These findings are presented in the next section.

## FINDINGS AND ANALYSIS

This section contains the findings and analysis of the case studies. Research interviews were conducted in February 2008.

## Company Background

Three organisations participated in the research and one project manager from each organisation was interviewed. One organisation did not wish to be named in this research, so the organisations are listed as Company A, B and C. Details of the participating organisations and the project managers interviewed are displayed in Table 2 below. Views are representative of the opinion of the project manager interviewed only.

|  | Company A | Company B | Company C |
|---|---|---|---|
| Industry of Organisation | Information Technology | Information Technology | Financial Services |
| No. of employees on site | 35 (on site) | 600(Ireland) | 185 (on site) |
| Years of experience as Project Manager | 2 | 11 | 6 |
| Years of experience managing Agile Projects | 12 | 5 | 10 months |

| No. of Agile Projects Managed | 2 | 3 with numerous releases. | 4 |
|---|---|---|---|
| Customers | External | Internal | Internal |
| Co located project teams | Yes | No | No |
| Agile Methodologies Used | XP (Customised) | XP (Customised) | Scrum & XP (Both Customised) |

*Table 2: Company and Project Manager Information*

The project manager interviewed in Company A manages a team consisting of four developers, and one tester. The team is made up of three senior and two junior people. In Company B the project manager currently manages a team of eight members, which consists of subject matter experts and individuals who represent business operations and IT personnel. Company C has a team director and technical architect based in the United States. The current project team consists of three team leads, two junior developers, a user interface designer, a business analyst, and an individual who looks after Quality Assurance.

## Project Planning and Scheduling

All three companies used the practise of time boxing in their projects. Company A, B and C set the duration of iterations as seen in Table 3 below.

| | Company A | Company B | Company C |
|---|---|---|---|
| Iteration Length in Days | 5-10 | 10 | 15 |

*Table 3: Iteration Length of each company.*

It was found that Company A vary their iteration size between 5-10 days depending on the project and how much work is involved compared to Companies B and C who use the same iteration length for all projects. The project manager in Company B stated that 5 days is to short because not enough product is achieved in that time period and felt that 15 days was to long. The project manager in Company C initially started with using 10 day iterations but struggled to produce meaningful functionality in that time period so the iterations were changed to 15 days.

All three companies used estimation before they start working on an iteration. In Company A their external customers discuss the requirements with the team and estimates are made using comparisons of previous pieces of work. In Company

B and C, where the customers are internal, estimation is a collaborative effort amongst the team.

Company C also estimates the size of a user story. This is done by means of a scale where a user story is given a certain number of points based on its size and work involved. For each iteration the points of all the user stories within an iteration are summed. Then the total points are compared to the natural velocity of Company C's 15 day iteration. For example, in Table 4 below, iteration X contains seven distinct user stories and the total point for the iteration is 65. The project manager knows from previous iterations that their natural velocity of iteration is 70 points so they are comfortable that iteration X will be completed in their 15 day iteration.

| Iteration X | Points |
|-------------|--------|
| User Story 1 | 5 |
| User Story 2 | 10 |
| User Story 3 | 6 |
| User Story 4 | 7 |
| User Story 5 | 15 |
| User Story 6 | 13 |
| User Story 7 | 9 |
| Total | 65 |

*Table 4: User Story Points*

The project managers in all three companies felt that agile estimation was more accurate than estimation methods used during a traditional SDLC. Agile estimation was tracked on a day-to-day basis where estimates are continuously assessed and improved by the project manager. In the case of Company C, the project manager meets with each developer on a daily basis and as a result this close, hands-on tracking of estimates resulted in increased control of the project as opposed to the traditional SDLC where estimates are given at the start of the project and may not be accessed until later stages of the project.

In all three companies requirements were prioritised by the customer. In Company A, where the customer is external, prioritisation is solely the responsibility of the customer. In companies B and C, where the customer is internal, the customer drives the prioritisation while input and feedback from the project team is taken on board and often results in changes in the prioritisation. It was noted by Company C, that it is the ideal for the customer to prioritise requirements as it leads to a more usable product, but customer involvement is not always possible where the project is technology driven.

## Team make-up

In all three companies, teams are chosen depending on the skill set required and who is available at the time. For all three companies the size of the team required depends on the project, the amount of functionality it requires, and the time and effort needed.

Company A finds it quite hard to divide up tasks as they lack experience, but the team use user stories as much as possible to help them. Company B and C have experts in each area working on the tasks. In company C, where the developers are very experienced in their areas, tasks are divided on the basis of expertise in a certain area and the manager monitors the tasks each member of the team is working on.

None of the companies interviewed experienced any resistance from team members when using agile methodologies.

## Communication

The project manager in Company A stated that the company manages communication by having weekly team meetings where the progress of development is discussed. The project manager in Company B stated that communication on agile projects varies from project to project and it is managed differently depending on whether the team is onsite for the project or distributed across different countries. Company C uses a variety of communication tools and technologies including instant messenger, audio and video conferencing. All three companies agreed that communication is much easier to manage when the team and the customer are co-located and acknowledge that face to face communication is the most effective means of communication when working on an agile project.

Company A finds face to face the most efficient way to communicate as there is better interaction between the team itself and between the team and the customer. In Company A, the project team is co-located so communication mostly is face to face along with email, and instant messenger.

Company B uses face to face communication where possible along with emails, documents, and conference calls. On their current project in Company B, the project team is spanning three countries in Europe and this poses a challenge for the team in how communication is handled amongst the team.

Company C's project team is not co-located. As team members are based in Ireland and the United States, daily stand up meetings take place at 4.45pm in Ireland so that it is a suitable time for team members in the United States. Company C finds that when communicating with team members in the States, it is best to use telephone conversations or video and audio conferencing to communicate with team members abroad and follow up these conversations with a summary of the conversation in an email for future reference.

Factors which affected communication were mainly due to different time zones and whether or not the project team and customer were co located. All three companies acknowledged that it is easier to manage an agile project when the team is co-located as communication can be face to face and instant.

Another issue which affected communication is culture differences and language barriers. Company B stated that not everyone's native language is English and that some times team members from other countries can have difficulties understanding what another team member has said or written.

The main differences in communication between an agile project and a traditional project are as follows: Company A stated that communication takes place on a more regular basis and it involves the customer more than on a traditional project; Company B found that communication was easier on an agile project and that communication is more verbal than written; and Company C also found that communication happens on a daily basis rather than every three to four days as it would have happened on a traditional project.

## Documentation

Company A manage their documentation through the use of a Sharepoint site and also through designing a project plan which contains user stories, releases and iterations. Each developer writes up the documentation which corresponds with the piece of functionality they are working on.

Company B had to meet IS9000 requirements, such as a development plan, test plan and design specification. In this company documentation was seen as a task to be completed rather than something which could be useful and the focus was on getting the documentation done and signed off rather than producing useful documentation.

The manager in Company C stated that his team struggled when it came to writing up documentation, so it was decided to write up the documentation at the end of a project. However, sometimes high level documentation is completed at the start, but generally the majority of the documentation, from a technical perspective, is done at the end. They feel that it is better to build something and then document it rather than document something and then build it, as requirements change and so do parts of functionality; which can result in documentation becoming out of date. The manager in Company C allows the people working on certain functionality to produce the documentation when their piece of functionality is finished and then the manager signs off on the documentation before it is sent off to the customer to be reviewed. Company C struggled with their documentation as they did not see it as a high priority.

All three companies strongly agreed that there was a much larger volume of documentation involved when working in a traditional project in comparison to an agile project.

## Post Implementation

All three companies were sceptical of agile methodologies from the outset. However, these perceptions changed as time went on and the people within the agile teams became more familiar with agile methodologies. In all three cases it is clear that the project manager preferred using an agile methodology to the traditional waterfall approach.

# DISCUSSION AND CONCLUSION

The purpose of this section is to discuss the findings and consider the conclusion from the research conducted. This section will conclude by considering the implications for practice.

## Discussion of Findings

On completing this research project, the project team found that there were similarities and differences between the existing literature and what was obtained from the project managers interviewed in relation to agile methodologies and project management.

After implementing agile methodologies, the project managers and the agile project team found that it improved communication and collaboration amongst project team members and documentation was light yet relevant.

Fitzgerald et al (2006) argue that Scrum and XP can be tailored and customised to suit different projects. The findings of this research concur with this as all three project managers were using customised versions of the methodologies to fit in with their organisational needs and management issues.

Larman (2004) states that iterations provide key stakeholders with greater visibility to the product throughout the development process, which encourages feedback and allows for more successful product development. This research found that visibility is not always apparent where projects are largely technology driven.

In the literature it stated that teams needed to be co-located (Ambler, 2002, pg 161 - 162). However, two of the three project managers interviewed had teams working across different regions. While the project managers admitted that it was not ideal for the project team to be dispersed, it still worked for them. Ambler (2002, pg 160 - 161) identifies that physical proximity can affect communication as the closer people are to one another then the greater the opportunities for effective communication. The findings concur with this as all project managers agreed that communication is much easier to manage when the team and customer are co-located and acknowledge that face to face communication is the most effective means of communication when working on an agile project.

Ambler (2002, pg 243) argues that all documentation should not be left towards the end. However, the findings show that documentation was seen as a task rather than something which could be useful. The focus was on getting the documentation done and signed off rather than producing useful documentation. As a result teams can struggle when it comes to writing up documentation so it was decided to write up the documentation at the end of a project.

**Implications for Practice**

It is hoped that this research will provide readers with an insight into managing software projects that use XP and Scrum from a project management perspective. This research obtains the opinions of project managers in relation to two agile methodologies and identifies what agile practices project managers are currently using in their organisations. As a result the findings in this research are limited somewhat, as it can only be applied to these two agile methodologies. Other organisations that use these agile methodologies may have different experiences to those related in this document. The four areas that were under investigation in the research were: project planning and scheduling; team selection; communication; and documentation. The research also identifies issues that organisations had when using an agile methodology. These issues may help other organisations to decide which agile methodology is most suitable to their needs.

## REFERENCES

Agile Alliance (2001)."Agile Alliance". Retrieved 14/12/2007, from
   www.agilealliance.org

Agile Manifesto (2001)."Agile Manifesto". Retrieved 13/12/2007, from
   www.agilemanifesto.org/history.html

Ambler, S. (2002) *Agile Modeling: Effective Practices for Extreme Programming and the Unified Process,* Wiley.

Cockburn, A. (2001) *"Agile Software Development ",* Cockburn & Highsmith Series
   Editors.

Cockburn, A. and Highsmith, J. (2001) "Agile Software Development: the business of innovation" *IEEE Computer,* **Vol 34**(9), pg 120.

Cohn., M. (2006) *Agile Estimating and Planning,* Prentice Hall.

Crushman, R. (1999) *The Standish Group -Chaos: A Recipe for Success..*

Duane, P. T., Richard, B. and Heinz, K. (1999) *"Growing systems in emergent organisations" Commun. ACM,* **Vol 42** (8), pg117-123.

Fitzgerald, B., Hartnett, G. and Conboy, K. (2006) *"Customising agile methods to software practices at Intel, Shannon", European Journal of Information Systems,* **Vol 15**, pg 200–213.

Hass, K. (2007) *"The Blending of Traditional and Agile Project Management", PM World Today,* **Vol 9** (5).

Highsmith, J. (2002) *Agile Software Development Ecosystems,* Addison Wesley.

Jalote, P., Palit, A., Kurien, P. and Peethamber, V. T. (2004), "Timeboxing: a process model for iterative software development", *Journal of Systems and Software,* **Vol 70** (1), pg 117-127.

Jefferies, R. A., Ann; Hendrickson, Chet (2001) *Extreme Programming Installed,* Prentice Hall PTR, , Upper Saddle River, NJ.

Larman, C. (2004) *"Agile and Iterative Development, A managers guide",* Addison-Wesley.

Leffingwell, D. and Muirhead, D. (2004) *"Tactical Management of Agile Development: Achieving Competitive Advantage"* In *Rally Software Development Corporation.*

Rising, L., Rising, L. and Janoff, N. S. (2000) *"The Scrum software devlopment process for small teams" Software, IEEE,* **Vol 17**(4), pg26-32.

Sanjiv, A., Bob, P., Fred, S. and Susan, W. (2005) "Agile project management:steering from the edges" *Commun. ACM,* **Vol 48** (12), pg 85-89.

Schwaber, K. (1995) *"Scrum Development Process"* In *Workshop on Business Object Design* OOPSLA'95.

Schwaber, K. and Beedle, M. (2002) *Agile Software Development with Scrum,* Prentice Hall.

Sridhar, N., RadhaKanta, M. and George, M. (2005) "Challenges of migrating to agile methodolgies" *Commun. ACM,* **Vol 48** (5), pg 72-78.

The Standish Group (1995) *"The Standish Group - Chaos".*

Williams, L., Williams, L. and Cockburn, A. (2003) "*Agile software development: it's about feedback and change*" *IEEE Computer,* Vol 36(6), pg 39-43.

# AN ALGORITHM OF DATA FUSION

Lei Qiu, School of Electronic Science and Engineering, National University of Defense Technology, Changsha, P.R.China, qiulei_2000@hotmail.com  (Student)

Xiangan Heng, School of Information System and Management, National University of Defense Technology, Changsha, P.R.China, xianganh@hotmail.com

Hao Wang, School of Electronic Science and Engineering, National University of Defense Technology, Changsha, P.R.China, whdave@sina.com(Supervisor)

## ABSTRACT

*Considering the characteristic of satellite integrated navigation, we improve the traditional algorithm of federal kalman filter and present an improved kalman filter algorithm when regional and global filters are designed according to different mathematics algorithms. The improved algorithm is then used in satellite integration navigation of GPS/INS/BD to make the navigation algorithm more suitable for the actual environment and more conventional.*

*Keywords: federal kalman filter, data fusion, integrated navigation.*

## INTRODUCTION

Data fusion [1] is a new developing technology currently which requires practice and is a process of data from different sensors in a system. As we all know, because any kind of sensor has its own disadvantages, there will be some disadvantages such as risks of error reporting, low stability and comprehension, if acquiring and processing data from a single sensor. The multi-sensor data fusion technology is developed to overcome such disadvantages and to have a correct, comprehensive cognition to the characteristic of measure environments or objects. Briefly speaking, multi-sensor date fusion technology [2] [3] integrates information from different sensors to calculate more reliable and accurate information than form single sensor. The frequent using methods of data fusion include Bayesian approach, D-S evidential theory and classic inferential algorithm. Some intelligent methods such as neutral network, wavelet analysis are also the widely using methods to research data fusion. Since kalman filter was presented in 1960s, it was widely used as a new filter in the research areas like controlling, tracking, and measuring, etc because of its best unbiased estimation for data estimation and simple structures. The centralized kalman filter which was widely used has to process the data from all the sensors has to calculate huge number of date and has a low real time ability and no capability for errors either. We present a filter which adapts different models based on federal kalman filter presented by Carlson and realize the optimal data fusion from multi-sensors. We argue that our system has the capability for errors and the adaptability is also well improved.

This paper is organized as follows. In section 2 we introduce the structure of classic federal kalman filter and the deduce process of the improved filter in which the regional and global filters are separately designed according to different mathematic algorithm. In section 3 we present how to apply the improved filter to GPS/INS/BD integrated navigation. In section 4, we simulate the algorithm above using matlab.

## IMPROVED FEDERAL KALMAN FILTER ALGORITHM

### Federal kalman filter

The design of federal kalman filter [4] is focus on 2 issues. One is processing the data separately and the other is fusing all the processed data together. To be specific, firstly we choose a filter which has comprehensive information and high reliability from all the sensors as a referenced filter. Then we ally this filter with the others one by one to construct some sub-filters which process data separately. Each sub-filter works according to the statement and measurement equations and outputs the optimal estimation results Xi, Pi, ( i= 1, 2, ⋯⋯n) based on regional measurements. These regional optimal estimations will be composed in the global filter according to the fusion algorithm and output the global estimation Xm, Pm. After each process of filtering, global filter will feedback to each regional filter with global result Xm and covariance matrix Pm which is formed according to the principles of information distribution to ensure a good capability of errors. Based on this idea, we conclude the structure of federal kalman filter (figure 1).

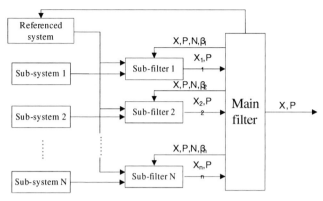

*Figure 1, structure of federal kalman filter*

## Improved federal kalman filter

Recently, to fuse information using federal kalman filter, regional and global filters always using the same model. However, considering in integrated navigation, the sub-systems may be various with different applying environments. We argue that the algorithm would be more actually if we adapt different statement variables for specific sub-systems according to the actual application. In another words, if regional and global filters are designed according to different models which are more specific with the application, the accuracy and generalization of system will be improved. Based on this consideration, we describe the regional and global filters which have different statement and measurement equations below.

The discrete model of global filter:

$$X(k+1)=\phi(k+1,k)X(k)+G(k+1)\,\mathrm{w}(k+1) \tag{1}$$

$$Z(k)=C(k)X(k)+\mathrm{v}(k) \tag{2}$$

In the model, $X(k)\in R^{n}$ is the statement variable of global filter; $\Phi(k+1,k)\in R^{n\times n}$ is the one step statement transfer matrix; $Z(k)\in R^{m}$ is the measurement vector; $C(k)\in R^{m\times n}$ is the measurement matrix; $\mathrm{w}(k)$ and $\mathrm{v}(k)$ are white noise sequence which independent with each other. $Q(k)$ and $R(k)$ are average and variance; the measurement variable includes all the measurement variables of sub-systems. $Z_{i}(k)\in R^{m_{i}}\,(i=1,2,\ldots,N)$, $m_{1}+m_{2}+\ldots\ldots m_{N}=m$, so:

$$Z(k)=\begin{bmatrix} Z_1(k) \\ Z_2(k) \\ \vdots \\ Z_N(k) \end{bmatrix}, C(k)=\begin{bmatrix} C_1(k) \\ C_2(k) \\ \vdots \\ C_N(k) \end{bmatrix}, R(k)=diag[R_1(k),R_2(k),\cdots R_N(k)]$$

If using centralized kalman filter, we can calculate globally optimal estimation of all observation value:

$$\hat{X}(k+1/k)=\Phi(k+1,k)\hat{X}(k) \tag{3}$$

$$P(k+1/k)=\Phi(k+1,k)P(k/k)\Phi^T(k+1,k)+G(k+1)Q(k+1)G^T(k+1) \tag{4}$$

$$K(k+1)=P(k+1/k)C^T(k+1)\left[C(k+1)P(k+1/k)C^T(k+1)+R(k+1)\right]^{-1} \tag{5}$$

$$\hat{X}(k+1/k+1)=\hat{X}(k+1/k)+K(k+1)\left[Z(k+1)-C(k+1)\hat{X}(k+1/k)\right]$$

$$=\left[I-K(k+1)C(k+1)\right]\hat{X}(k+1/k)+K(k+1)Z(k+1)$$

$$=\left[I-\sum_{i=1}^{N}K_i(k+1)C_i(k+1)\right]\Phi(k+1,k)\hat{X}(k/k)+\sum_{i=1}^{N}K_i(k+1)Z_i(k+1)$$

$$=A(k+1)\hat{X}(k/k)+\sum_{i=1}^{N}K_i(k+1)Z_i(k+1) \tag{6}$$

Among them:

$$A(k+1)=\left[I-\sum_{i=1}^{N}K_i(k+1)C_i(k+1)\right]\Phi(k+1,k) \tag{7}$$

$$K_i(k+1)Z_i(k+1)=\left[I+P(k+1/k)C_i^T(k+1)R_i^{-1}(k+1)C_i(k+1)\right]^{-1}$$

$$P(k+1/k)C_i^T(k+1)R^{-1}(k+1)Z_i(k+1) \tag{8}$$

$$P(k+1/k+1)=\left[I-K(k+1)C(k+1)\right]P(k+1/k) \tag{9}$$

If there are N sub-systems, there are N regional filters specific with sub-systems. The mathematic model is below:

$$X_i(k+1)=\Phi_i(k+1,k)X_i(k)+G_i(k+1)w_i(k+1) \tag{10}$$

$$Z_i(k+1)=H_i(k+1)X_i(k+1)+v_i(k+1) \tag{11}$$

also:     $$C_i(k+1)=H_i(k+1)S_i(k+1) \quad i=1,2,\cdots,N \tag{12}$$

The regional filter adapts the optimal estimation algorithm of kalman filter, so similarly,

$$\hat{X}_i(k+1/k+1)=A_i(k+1)\hat{X}_i(k/k)+K_{Li}(k+1)Z_i(k+1) \tag{13}$$

$$A_i(k+1)=\left[I-K_i(k+1)H_i(k+1)\right]\Phi_i(k+1,k) \tag{14}$$

$$K_{Li}(k+1)=\left[I+P_i(k+1/k)H_i^T(k+1)R_i^{-1}(k+1)H_i(k+1)\right]^{-1}$$

$$P_i(k+1/k)H_i^T(k+1)R_i^{-1}(k+1) \tag{15}$$

$$P_i(k+1/k)=\Phi_i(k+1,k)P_i(k/k)\Phi_i^T(k+1,k)+G_i(k+1)Q_i(k+1)G_i^T(k+1) \tag{16}$$

Then we input the optimal estimations of each regional filter to the second level filter, and the global filter accomplishes information fusion. According to (13), we can acquire:

$$K_{Li}(k+1)Z_i(k+1)=\hat{X}_i(k+1/k+1)-A_i(k+1)\hat{X}_i(k/k) \tag{17}$$

We input (15) into (17) and transform it by left multiplication, then:

$$P_i(k+1/k)H_i^T(k+1)R_i^{-1}(k+1)Z_i(k+1)$$
$$=\left[I+P_i(k+1/k)H_i^T(k+1)R_i^{-1}(k+1)H_i(k+1)\right]$$
$$\left[\hat{X}_i(k+1/k+1)-A_i(k+1)\hat{X}_i(k/k)\right] \tag{18}$$
$$H_i^T(k+1)R_i^{-1}(k+1)Z_i(k+1)=\left[P_i^{-1}(k+1/k)+H_i^T(k+1)R_i^{-1}(k+1)H_i(k+1)\right]$$
$$\left[\hat{X}_i(k+1/k+1)-A_i(k+1)\hat{X}_i(k/k)\right] \tag{19}$$

Inputting (12) and (19) into (8), so:

$$K_i(k+1)Z_i(k+1)=\left[I+P(k+1/k)C_i^T(k+1)R_i^{-1}(k+1)C_i(k+1)\right]^{-1}$$
$$P(k+1/k)S_i^T(k+1)H_i^T(k+1)R_i^{-1}(k+1)Z_i(k+1)$$
$$=\left[I+P(k+1/k)C_i^T(k+1)R_i^{-1}(k+1)C_i(k+1)\right]^{-1}$$
$$P(k+1/k)S_i^T(k+1)$$
$$\left[P_i^{-1}(k+1/k)+H_i^T(k+1)R_i^{-1}(k+1)H_i(k+1)\right]$$
$$\left[\hat{X}_i(k+1/k+1)-A_i(k+1)\hat{X}_i(k/k)\right]$$
$$=F_i(k+1)\left[\hat{X}_i(k+1/k+1)-A_i(k+1)\hat{X}_i(k/k)\right] \tag{20}$$

In (20),

$$F_i(k+1)=\left[I+P(k+1/k)C_i^T(k+1)R_i^{-1}(k+1)C_i(k+1)\right]$$
$$P(k+1/k)S_i^T(k+1)$$
$$\left[P_i^{-1}(k+1/k)+H_i^T(k+1)R_i^{-1}(k+1)H_i(k+1)\right] \tag{21}$$
$$=P(k+1/k+1)S_i^T(k+1)P_i^{-1}(k+1/k+1)$$

Then input (20) into (6),

$$\hat{X}(k+1/k+1)=A(k+1)\hat{X}(k/k)+\sum_{i=1}^{N}F_i(k+1)\left[\hat{X}_i(k+1/k+1)-A_i(k+1)\hat{X}_i(k/k)\right]$$
$$=\xi(k+1/k+1)+\sum_{i=1}^{N}F_i(k+1)\hat{X}_i(k+1/k+1) \tag{22}$$

In the equation:

$$\xi(k+1/k+1)=A(k+1)\hat{X}_i(k/k)-\sum_{i=1}^{N}F_i(k+1)A_i(k+1)\hat{X}_i(k/k) \tag{23}$$

Then input $\hat{X}_i(k/k)=\xi(k/k)+\sum_{i=1}^{N}F_i(k)\hat{X}_i(k/k)$ into (23), so:

$$\xi(k+1/k+1)=A(k+1)\left[\xi(k/k)+\sum_{i=1}^{N}F_{i}(k)\hat{X}_{i}(k/k)\right]-\sum_{i=1}^{N}F_{i}(k+1)A_{i}(k+1)\hat{X}_{i}(k/k)$$

$$=A(k+1)\xi(k/k)+\sum_{i=1}^{N}\left[A(k+1)F_{i}(k)-F_{i}(k+1)A_{i}(k+1)\right]\hat{X}_{i}(k/k)$$

$$=A(k+1)\xi(k/k)+\sum_{i=1}^{N}T_{i}(k+1)\hat{X}_{i}(k/k) \tag{24}$$

In (24):

$$T_{i}(k+1)=\left[A(k+1)F_{i}(k)-F_{i}(k+1)A_{i}(k+1)\right] \tag{25}$$

So we can conclude the information fusion algorithm of global filter below:

$$\hat{X}(k+1/k+1)=\xi(k+1/k+1)+\sum_{i=1}^{N}F_{i}(k+1)\hat{X}_{i}(k+1/k+1) \tag{26}$$

$$\xi(k+1/k+1)=A(k+1)\xi(k/k)+\sum_{i=1}^{N}T_{i}(k+1)\hat{X}_{i}(k/k) \tag{27}$$

$$F_{i}(k+1)=P(k+1/k+1)S_{i}^{T}(k+1)P_{i}^{-1}(k+1/k+1) \tag{28}$$

$$T_{i}(k+1)=A(k+1)F_{i}(k)-F_{i}(k+1)A_{i}(k+1) \tag{29}$$

$$A(k+1)=\left[I-\sum_{i=1}^{N}M_{i}(k+1)C_{i}(k+1)\right]\Phi_{i}(k+1,k) \tag{30}$$

$$K_{i}(k+1)=P(k+1/k)C_{i}^{T}(k+1)\left[C_{i}(k+1)P(k+1/k)C_{i}^{T}(k+1)+R_{i}(k+1)\right]^{-1} \tag{31}$$

$$P(k+1/k)=\Phi(k+1,k)P(k/k)\Phi^{T}(k+1,k)+G(k+1)Q(k+1)G^{T}(k+1) \tag{32}$$

$$P(k+1/k+1)=\left[I-\sum_{i=1}^{N}K_{i}(k+1)C_{i}(k+1)\right]P(k+1/k) \tag{33}$$

# USING IMPROVED FEDERAL KALMAN FILTER IN GPS/INS/BD INTEGRATED NAVIGATION

## Principles of integrated navigation

There are many combinations among GPS/INS/BD, 2 of them are usually used. One is the combination of location and speed. GPS, INS and BD separately dynamic calculate the locations and synchronize them; then we use the subtractions of locations and speeds between GPS and INS, and between BD and INS as the measurement vectors of filter. At last, we use kalman filter to get the optimal estimations of errors of locations, speeds and other parameters of integrated navigation, and revise the three systems separately. This combination can compress the size of data, but in another way, it loses a lot of original data.

The other combination [6] is between pseudorange and pseudorange rate [5]. We directly combine the original observation information which generally means pseudorange, pseudorange rate of GPS and DB with INS. Receivers gain the sample data by abstracting original pseudorange and pseudorange rate. Then using the observation satellite ephemeris, we map the cumulative errors to the sight distance errors from users to satellites and filtering according to the residual error between pseudorange and pseudorange rate to acquire the estimation of error statement. This combination keeps important original data and improves the filter accuracy, but it causes low runtime speed. Our paper adapts the second combination.

## Applying improved federal kalman filter in GPS/INS/BD integrated navigation

The statement equation of GPS/INS regional filter is below:

$$\dot{X}(t) = F(t)X(t) + G(t)W(t) \tag{35}$$

In the equation, X is the error statement vector,

$$X = [\delta r_E, \delta r_N, \delta r_U, \delta v_E, \delta v_N, \delta v_U, \phi_E, \phi_N, \phi_U, \varepsilon_{bx}, \varepsilon_{by}, \varepsilon_{bz}, \varepsilon_{rx}, \varepsilon_{ry}, \varepsilon_{rz}, \nabla_x, \nabla_y, \nabla_z, \delta t_u \delta t_{ru}] \tag{36}$$

E, N, U separately mean three axes of east, north and up; $\delta r_E, \delta r_N, \delta r_U$ are location errors, $\delta v_E, \delta v_N, \delta v_U$ are speed errors, $\phi_E, \phi_N, \phi_U$ are platform error angles; $\varepsilon_{bx}, \varepsilon_{by}, \varepsilon_{bz}$ are random gyro replacement; $\varepsilon_{rx}, \varepsilon_{ry}, \varepsilon_{rz}$ are gyro first order makov errors; $\nabla_x, \nabla_y, \nabla_z$ are acceleration errors; $\delta t_u$ is the distance error caused by GPS clock error; $\delta t_{ru}$ is the speed error caused by GPS clock error; $F(t)$ is a 20 plus 20 matrix, which is defined by the error matrix of ins, the model of gyro replacement, and the system error matrix of GPS; $W(t)$ is the system noise.

The observation equation of GPS/INS regional filter is below,

$$Z_1(t) = H_1 X_1(t) + V_1(t) \tag{37}$$

$$Z_1(t) = \begin{bmatrix} \delta\rho \\ \delta\dot{\rho} \end{bmatrix} = \begin{bmatrix} \rho_1 - \rho_G \\ \dot{\rho}_1 - \dot{\rho}_G \end{bmatrix} \tag{38}$$

$H_1$ is the observation matrix; $V_1(t)$ is the observation noise of pseudorange and its transformation rate. We discrete (35) (37):

$$X(k) = \Phi(k.k-1)X(k-1) + \Gamma(k-1)W(k-1) \tag{39}$$

$$Z_1(k) = H_1(k)X_1(k) + V_1(k) \tag{40}$$

In (21), $\Phi(k,k-1)$ is the statement transformation matrix from $t_{k-1}$ to $t_k$.

Similarly, the statement vector and equation of sub-filters combined by INS and BD are similar with the statement vector and equation of sub-filters combined by GPS/INS. The measurement equation is below,

$$Z_2(t_k) = H_2 X_2(t_k) + V_2(t_k) \tag{41}$$

$Z_2(t_k)$ is the subtraction between pseudorange and pseudorange rate of INS and BD, $H_2$ is observation matrix, $V_2(t)$ is the observation noise of pseudorange and pseudorange rate.

Finally, we can acquire the global estimation according to the fusion algorithm based on kalman filter we describe above, see below:

$$\hat{X}(k) = E\left[X(k)/Z_1(j), \cdots Z_k(j), j=1,\cdots,k\right]$$

## EXPERIMENT AND ANALYZE

To evaluate the effects of improved federal kalman filter we present above, we design a simulation experiment using matlab which simulates how it works in GPS/INS/BD integrated navigation system. We set the parameters below: Latitude is 40.56°; longitude is 0°; the initialize course error is 0.5°, gyro replacement is 0.001°per hour; sampling cycle is 300s; N is 10. According to the fusion algorithm above, we draw the simulation curve below (figure 2, figure 3). Blue line means the observation curve of errors in x and y directions; broken line stands the original filter curve and red line means the improved filter curve.

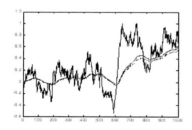     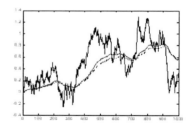

*Figure 2, simulation curve of x direction*          *Figure 3, simulation curve of y direction*

Seeing from the two figures, we can conclude that in the same initial conditions, the improved federal kalman filter we present in this paper is better than classic federal kalman filter. The improved filter reduces the errors of navigation parameters, rapidly converged, and more accuracy. So this new filter will be effective to improve the accuracy and reliability of integrated navigation.

## REFERENCES

[1]Xurong, D., Shouxin, Z., Zhongchun, H. (1998). GPS/INS integrated navigation and its application [M]. Changsha, *Press of National University of Defense Technology.*

[2]R.C.Luo,L .M,scherp. Dynamic Multi-sensor Data Fusion System for Intelligent Robots. *IEEE Journal of Robotics and Automation,1988,4(4)*: *386-389*

[3]J.Leopoldo, S.Longhi, G.Venturini. Development and Experimental Vallidation of an Adaptive Extended Kalman Filter for Localization of Mobile Robots. *IEEE Transactions on Robotics and Automation.1999,15(2):219-229.*

[4]Yongyuan, Q., Hongyue, Z., Shuhua, W. (1998). Principles of Kalman filter and integrated navigation [M]. Xi'an, *Press of University of Northwesten industry.*

[5]Wenxian, Y., Shaowei, Y., Guirong, G. (1994). Information fusion technologies from multiple sensors [J]. *Journal of National University of Defense Technology, 16(4)*: *1-11*

[6]Jing, Y., Hongyue, Z., Shiqing, Z. (2003). An error comprehensive integrated navigation system of GPS/SINS based on pseudorange and pseudorange rate [J]. *Journal of spaceflight control, 3*: *17-25.*

# PROJECT AND QUALITY MANAGEMENT IN A STUDENT SOFTWARE DEVELOPMENT PROJECT

Florian Moser, Faculty of Business Administration, University of Augsburg, 86153 Augsburg, Germany, Florian.Gerhard.Moser@Student.uni-augsburg.de
Tel: +49 177 46 19 48 4

## ABSTRACT

*This paper is about project management in a student software development project. The goal was to develop a web based job administration tool for the managing director of the business administration faculty at the University of Augsburg, Germany. The project was part of a software development seminar attended by 12 students from the fields of informatics and business administration. The students were supervised by a research assistant and a project manager from the TÜV IT Germany. The paper illustrates how the project management team used tools and instruments to control and manage the different teams during the project. It focuses on the role of quality management during the development progress and how it was applied. Moreover, arising problems in the project phase and lessons learned are shown in this essay. Since the author was one of the project managers, mainly responsible for quality management and tests, this paper focuses on these issues.*

*Keywords: Software Engineering, Project Management, Software Quality Management*

## INTRODUCTION AND PROBLEM SETTING

At the Business Administration faculty in the University of Augsburg, approximately 200 people are employed as professors, secretaries, research assistants or lecturers. Due to a complex system of distributing positions to the employees, e. g. having positions paid by the federal state, third party funds, project work etc., the task of matching employees to the right positions is quite difficult. Additionally, not every position is a full position. For some positions only ¼, ½ or ¾ of the full salary is paid or contracts have different expiration dates. Furthermore, it is possible that employees change along the positions they get their salary for. The executive director of the faculty, who has to organise the matching of persons, positions, time and several other constraints, uses spread sheets and handwritten documents to manage this task. Doing it in this way is highly complex, static and manually driven. Therefore it is very time-consuming, error-prone and, since only a few persons are in this work, not easy assignable to others. Since the faculty managing director's area of responsibility has grown significantly during the past few years, the cost-benefit ratio of the manual administration got out of the line. As a consequence, he gave the chair of business administration, information systems science and financial engineering the mandate to evaluate the possibilities of developing individual software that could come up against this problem. The chair assigned this project to a group of students who were attending a seminar about software development and project management. This paper describes the software development process from the project management's point of view, due to the fact that the author himself was a member of the project management team, which was responsible for the organisation of the project. In fact, this situation reflects a real life situation, in which a project sponsor (the managing director of the faculty) has a business driven need that has to be solved by using information technology, while the project team has the task to fulfil the business needs.

After describing the general setting and aim of the project, the composition of the project team and the time horizon, the main section of this paper will concern the role of the project management. This team had to coordinate the teams and their collaboration among each other. The next section gives an introduction to the team settings and compositions Section three illustrates how the project management team arranged the administration and communication of the project, whereas section four focuses on how the team ensured a high quality of both the software development process and the software itself. Section five describes the problems, the team had to cope with, while the last section gives an idea, what valuable experiences the students gained from this project and that lessons they learned.

## PROJECT AND TEAM SETTINGS

The very first step of the project was the project kick off where the students, the managing director and the project supervisors met for the first time. In this kick off, the students were introduced into the actual set of problems and the business needs. The managing director, in the following called customer, set the team the task to develop a web based solution that should be able to support his team in the job mapping process by means of a dynamic and reliable job administration tool. Since the customer also works at home on a regular basis, he emphasized a web based solution as the only must criteria. According to their abilities and experiences, the students were separated into several teams, which will be introduced in the following. The teams also got professional support from a research assistant and from a project manager of the TÜV IT Germany. The latter gave hints as how to face problems and what methods could be useful for this purpose. As a time horizon, the students had about ten weeks, while the distribution of the time to the different teams was arranged as follows.

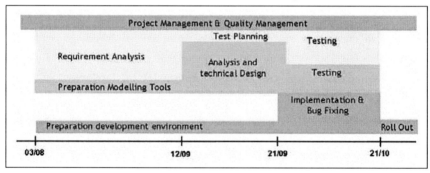

*Figure 1. The timeline of the project with the different development phases*

## Project Management

This team consisted of two students from the field of business administration. They had the superior challenge to coordinate the whole development process, from the first customer contact to the roll out of the software, as well as the whole quality management process. Given that the central aspect of this paper is to reflect the work and methods by this team, more details about work and solutions will be discussed later on.

## Requirements Analysis

A fundamental and correct requirements analysis is one of the most critical success drivers in a software project, resulting in being the most time consuming phase. Especially in a software project that has such a restricted time plan this task plays a decisive role, a fact that was a reason for the bigger size of the team. The team, dealing with this subject, consisted of two students with business administration background and two from the field of informatics. This composition guaranteed both a business and a technical view to ensure a well-founded analysis of the customer's requirements. The final task of the team was to develop a requirement specification including textual descriptions of the problem, graphical Use Case Diagrams as well as Activity Diagrams of the business processes the software should reproduce. The following figure shows the original Use Case Diagram, taken from the requirement analysis of the software project.

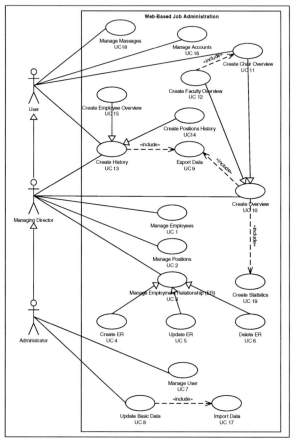

*Figure 2. The Use-Case Diagram of the software as an example for the requirement analysis.*

## Analysis and Design

After completing the business requirements analysis, it was up to the next team to translate these documents into a technical view to provide a framework the coding team could start to work with. The task of this team, consisting of three students, and also multidisciplinary in its composition, was to create Class Diagrams, Interaction Diagrams and, in order to ensure a solid data base for the software, an Entity Relationship Model that is shown exemplarily in the following.

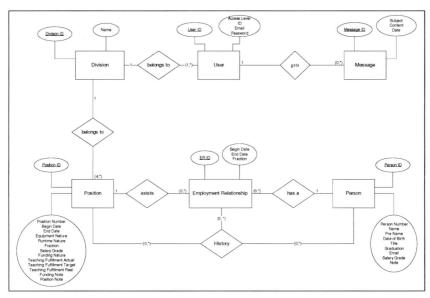

*Figure 3. The Entity-Relationship Model of the software as an example for the technical analysis.*

## Implementation

After the entire analysis and modelling work was completed, the actual coding was started by three informatics students to whom it was now up to create the software by using all the preliminary work, done by the other teams.

## Test

This team was formed out of the Analysis and Design Team and one member of the Requirements Analysis Team, as developing coders should not test their own work. How the tests were organised is described latter on and therefore not part of this paragraph.

## Quality Management

To ensure a high level of software quality, the project management team also controlled the quality of both the development process and the software by providing measures that should ensure quality in the project. Details about this process are illustrated in a later paragraph.

# ORGANIZATION OF COMMUNICATION AND DOCUMENTATION

Subsequent to the project kick off, the project management team had time to study useful methods to organise the development of software within a team, and finally agreed on three main tasks it had to handle.

## Organizing communication and documentation

Ensuring the communication between the project members was one of the most challenging tasks the project management team had to deal with, since the team was working heavily distributed and not in a full time environment. Consequently, it was up to the project management team to provide solutions to enable communication channels. For centralised document storage, a shared network directory with different areas for the teams was installed, where the teams could store their artefacts so that other members could access them. After evaluating the most useable and free available communication media, contact lists with e-Mail addresses, mobile phone numbers and instant messenger conferences were decided to be used as electronical devices next to personal meetings. For written communication in e-Mails, the project management team established communication rules to guarantee easy readable and understandable messages. The project management team also looked up methods for how to avoid problems like redundant communication and misunderstandings, described in well-established literature (Henrich 2002). As a result, the project management team decided to create a one to one contact person culture where each subproject team had one speaker and this speaker had one person within the project management team he or she could appeal to, if needed (Zuser et al. 2001). In addition, a contact person between the teams was established. This was necessary since the project management team wanted to ensure a permanent communication between the teams to avoid isolated development of one team without the next team's input. These interface persons had the task to communicate with the prior team on a regular basis to guarantee that following teams would be able to understand and use the prior team's work. Next to these communication channels, the project management team established regular team meetings with both the different teams and the entire project team. These meetings should provide a platform for the teams to present and discuss their current work, upcoming challenges, problems, and to inform the team about important issues, deadlines, milestones etc.

To ensure a latter traceability and justification, the well-founded documentation of decisions and artefacts was another task the project management team had to deal with.

During the ten weeks of project, the project management team was holding an official internal meeting twice a week, as well as about 35 meetings with other project teams that needed to be recorded and documented. For this reason, the team developed a protocol sheet, that logged all relevant information like attendees, time, decisions, information, tasks, the responsible person as well as forecasts and conclusions according to well-established literature (Zuser et al. 2001). From day one all project teams were familiarised with this protocol style. The project management team also urged the teams to log all meetings with the relevant information and hand it in regularly, a step that supported the project supervision significantly. As another tool, central open issue lists, which were also available for the project management team, were introduced in every team to guarantee a permanent view over delays and responsibilities within the developing teams. Within the shared directory, the management set up rules as to how documents should be named ("YYMMDD Name V00.01") and filed to enable an easy crawling through all the documents on the central document server. These measures guaranteed that the project management team had a permanent overview over finalised documents and all consistent documents logging the interaction between teams during the development process.

## Evaluating milestones and dependencies between tasks

At the very beginning of the project, it was up to the project management team to identify the milestones of the development process as a basis for the latter project plan. Hence, several meetings took place between the project management team and the developing teams in order to evaluate the content of the different team's work, their milestones and the dependencies in time between them. Thus, in cooperation with the teams, the project management team developed a diagram that is to illustrate the actual status of developed documents, the target state and all activities in between which had to be completed to reach the next milestone (Zuser et al. 2001). For the development of the actual project plan, this was the basis of discussion for each team's deliveries and final milestones, since it helped to evaluate, what activities had to be done in which order. Of course, during the project time several aspects changed and therefore had to be regularly adapted in the project plan.

Once the project management team had evaluated which activities would be necessary for the software development, a work break down structure had to be developed, that demonstrated the distribution of activities among the different teams. The team therefore used a top down approach to break down the whole project into more detailed activities, which had been identified beforehand, in order to reduce the complexity of the project (Project Management Blog 2007). As a result, the project management team provided an overview of all activities and the responsible team in each case, which is shown in the following.

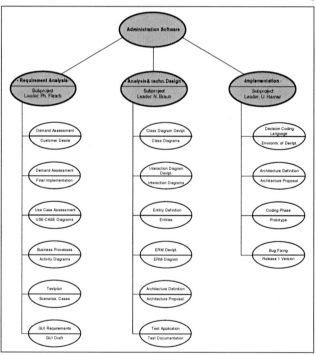

*Figure 4. The Work Break Down Structure of the development progress.*

## Drawing up a project plan to supervise and control the project

By completing the evaluation of activities and milestones, the project management team was now able to develop a project plan that included all the aspects required to control and monitor the project. This tool now showed the workings, the timeline, the responsible teams and the dependencies between the activities. As well as other control documents, the project plan was adapted frequently to react on delays or changes in the customer requirements. Therefore, the project management team was always able to show the actual status of the project to the customer as well as to the teams and supervisors. Bottlenecks in resource planning, critical delays or long term risks in the project evolution could be identified early and adequate measures could be defined, controlled and arranged. In regular discussions with the teams, the project plan was aligned to current challenges, changes, and consequently turned out to be the most important supervising and controlling instrument (Steinweg 2005). To show the structure of the project plan, the following figure provides an excerpt of it.

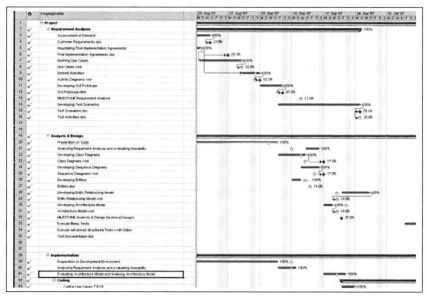

*Figure 5. An excerpt of the project plan.*

Even with these controlling tools, the project management team faced one serious challenge while planning the project: Estimating the time the different teams would have to develop their milestones. Though the general timeline was given by the project supervisors, the fine tuning turned out to be more complicated than expected. One main reason for that was the lack of any experience from earlier projects, within the project management team. Consequently, the project plan had to be thrown over several times in order to react on delays which were unpredictable and unscheduled, respectively, during the project time. Without a well-founded project plan, the accomplishment of the project would not have been possible, as the team also had to ensure high quality in the process of software development, whereby the project plan also was a useful tool. Other tools and measures, the project management team used to guarantee a high quality in this project, are described in the following paragraph.

## QUALITY MANAGEMENT

In industries like care manufacturing, quality management plays a significant role since decades. Software industry also should apply these aspects, but since it is as a quite young industry producing intangible goods, it needs its own quality aspects. For this industry, it is important to achieve customer satisfaction through high quality in both the software development process and the final software itself. For this reason, the project management distinguished between development process quality aspects and the quality of the final product, since the first part directly influences the second one.

There are different approaches how to define the quality of software. As an example, according to the DIN standard, the quality of software is measurable in how the attributes meet the requirements and expectations originally agreed on (DIN 55350 & DIN ISO 9126). Since there are also some other different views on quality, the team first had to decide what quality approach to pursue, given that in literature several approaches are proposed for different software types. Seeing that this software project did not aim at a mass product but at individual software, a "user-orientated approach" (Balzert 1998) seemed to fit the conditions of this project best. The team agreed on this approach, since this approach's "fitness-for-use" aim targets on meeting the customer's requirements first. Ironically, the customer did not have any detailed quality requirements. Consequently, the team decided to follow a second quality approach, namely "process-orientated quality approach" (Balzert 1998). In contrast to the first approach, this is about reaching high quality of the final product through a high quality in the development process. The target is to avoid later effort in repairing and extra work through detailed specification and control of the processes. Consequently, the team's challenge was to provide measures that would guarantee a high quality of the end product, as well as of the process of development itself. For this reason, a quality management framework, based on a one used in practice (Balzert 1998), was evolved, that covered both aspects in one framework. This five step framework then was used throughout the entire project and is presented in the following subsection.

In a first step of the framework, the quality requirements had to be evaluated and cleared with the customer before secondly, measurable quality target agreements were defined. These quality agreements represented the quality the team had to deliver at the end of the project. In a third step, a catalogue of instruments was developed to document all measures the quality management team took to reach the quality agreements. These instruments were used in the fourth step, the quality steering. The first four steps illustrate how the team tried to fulfil the "process-oriented quality approach" to ensure a high quality of the process. In order to reach a high quality in the "fitness-for-use" approach, a fifth step tested all building blocks of the software against the requirements, to guarantee a high standard of the product itself. Figure 6 depicts the five steps, which are described in more detail below.

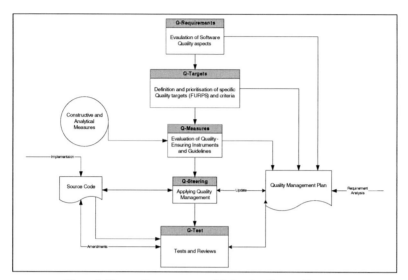

*Figure 6. The quality process model showing five quality steps.*

## Step 1&2: Evaluation and definition of quality targets

After a series of interviews with the customer, it turned out that, besides usability, the customer did not have any specific quality requirements. Hence, the customer asked the project management team to look about quality targets used in practice that could also suit this project. Consequently, the team read up on different techniques and came across the so called "FURPS-Model", applied by Hewlett-Packard, which covers the quality aspects Functionality, Usability, Reliability, Performance and Supportability (Balzert 1998). **F**unctionality as the umbrella term for correctness and security; **U**sability standing for comprehensibility and general ergonomic aspects; **R**eliability as factor for restorability as well as maturity; **P**erformance that stands for response time and resources needed; **S**upportability with the criteria how easy the software is to be modified and extendable.

These five quality factors were discussed within the project team as well as with the customer, to get a weighting and a priority list, since some factors might negatively influence others (e. g. Usability may negatively influence Performance but, since only one person would be using the software and a user-oriented approach was applied, Usability was privileged). As a result, the priority for the software was decided as follows: Functionality – Usability – Reliability – Supportability – Performance. According to this quality target priority, the project team developed the software and tested it later on.

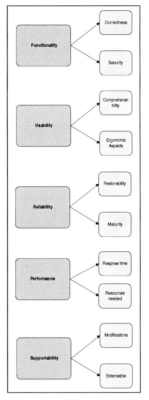

*Figure 7. The software quality factors derived from the "FURPS" quality model.*

## Step 3&4: Defining and applying a catalogue of quality ensuring measures

In order to control the quality within the software development project, the project management team developed a catalogue with instruments and guidelines to ensure a high quality of the process of software development, as well as for the software. This was necessary to fulfil the quality targets earlier agreed on by the project team and the customer. Those instruments and guidelines can be divided into so- called "constructive measures" and "analytical measures", whereby the first are to ensure "a priori" high quality in process and product, whereas the latter ones do not enhance the quality essentially. The analytical measures actually measure the level of the current quality to proof against the quality agreements with the intention to order an enhancement (Balzert 1998). To illustrate the idea of this structure, two examples per group are described in more detail below, whereas the figure shows an overview over all instruments applied.

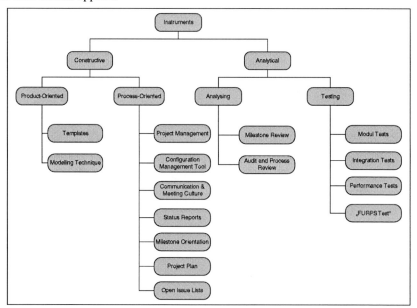

*Figure 8. Catalogue of instruments applied in quality management.*

## Constructive Measures

Within the constructive measures, the project management team distinguished between instruments that should enhance the product's quality and those which should reach the quality for the process. As an example for the first one, the team agreed on UML (Unified Modelling Language) as the only language to model diagrams, since, in this manner, misunderstandings could be avoided. For the process enhancement, the well-founded project plan has to be cited, since this instrument managed the whole project process end-to-end and therefore guaranteed a well-founded process controlling.

*Analytical Measures*

Within the analytical measures, there also has to be distinguished between two different types of instruments. Regular reviews, as an example for more analysing methods, ensured a nonstop control of documents, milestones or code fractions to be able to react on upcoming problems at an early stage.

Integration-Tests, as an example for the testing types of instruments, were focused on the software during the test phase, where the team tested the software as an entire product.

## Step 5: Reviews and Tests

During the project phase, all milestones (e. g. Requirement Analysis or Technical Analysis) were taken under review, where the project management team and one representative of each team proofread the milestone thoroughly. During this process the reviewer put their remarks in a review template and discussed the findings in a review meeting with the team that had developed the milestone. The team responsible for the milestone inserted the annotations and, after a re-review, the milestone was marked as approved and so the next milestone could be developed. This procedure guaranteed a high quality in the developing process, since all teams agreed on every milestone and so the success depended on everyone. The work of the project management team itself was also reviewed regularly in form of surveys within the project team, to disclose discrepancies or management failures in the project. Reviews therefore granted quality in both the processes and the milestones leading to the software product itself.

Compared to the regular reviews of documents, the entire test activities can be characterised as more dynamic, since there has been interaction between all the teams. The test phase was divided in different sections such as "module testing", i. e. testing several code fragments only. These tests were arranged by the implementation team and did not follow a structured scenario. "Integration and system tests", in contrast, were accomplished according to a structured test scenario the Requirement Analysis team had developed in order to test all business requirements. These test scenarios, which included detailed guidelines on how to test the functions of the software, were stored in a web based "bug tracking tool". This allowed the testers to execute the tests they were responsible for, step by step, and to add different kinds of defects with a description (e. g. "blemish" or "function unavailable") into the tool. The coding team on the other side received the automatically generated messages about defects and the connected test cases and therefore was able to fix these according to the priority the tester had classified the defects in. In regular meetings with the project management team (so called "Issue Management Meetings"), the testers and developers discussed the defects and how to deal with them. Depending on the prominence of a defect, the project management team decided whether to drop off a function (if compatible with the customer requirements) or to generate a "change request" that had to be discussed with the customer, since it had implications on hitherto existing requirements and quality aspects and, in a few cases, also on functions in the software. The test phase continued until the project deadline was reached and all defects, aside from a few "nice to have" functions, were fixed. In the last "Roll out test", the entire software was tested along all the "FURPS" factors and afterwards was ready for the handover to the customer, who also got a manual and training course about how to use the software and its features.

## PROBLEMS

Considering the fact that this project was realised by students with no software development practice at all, the achievements and the process itself can be considered as very satisfactory. Even so, as in practice, some problems occurred that should not be left unmentioned, since they were quite similar problems as in real life software projects. Exemplarily, three of these problems are illustrated in the following.

## Lack of communication

As (software) projects are heavily driven by interaction between people, adequate communication is a crucial success factor. The project management team soon had to face the problem that the teams did not communicate enough with the project management team and neither within the team itself. Consequently, important information did not obtain the persons needing it in the required time, which lead to misunderstandings, dispensable extra work or disputes between and within teams. Additionally, the supervision by the project management team became more difficult since all the work of planning and controlling was based on information flow to forecast the development.

## Lack of documentation

Software development brings with it large amounts of documentation, as all decisions of meetings, evaluations of possibilities or the software code itself have to be documented to make the process and the product comprehensible for later users. Even though one focus of the project management's concern was to guarantee a well-founded documentation, this task unfortunately did not reach its goal completely what lead to some lacks in documentation. This came with the fact that even though, measures like records drafts, several guidelines and rules had been implemented, the teams did not keep up with these during the entire process.

## Questions of authority

Leading a (student) project in the role of a project manager also turned out to be a challenge of moderating between team members, who did not always have enough trust in the other team's work, and competencies. Therefore, regular arguments on issues like modeling- and coding methodologies, applied instruments or ways of how to lead the project appeared and disturbed the atmosphere and development progress.

# CONCLUSION

Being part of this project was a unique opportunity for all the students to gain very important project work experience. Especially the possibility to work together in multidisciplinary teams gave them the chance to interact with students with different backgrounds in study and experience. Even if this constellation in particular sometimes lead to dissensions between the team members, this experience will help all the students to act and react better in projects in their later career. For the project management team, this was an invaluable experience in how to manage a project and how to lead a team in particular. The experience how to face conflicts may help the members of this team to react more calmly in later situations in professional work situations. The students also gained valuable methodological skills in using project management tools and methods. Since this project was part of a project seminar, the students had the possibility to compare the theoretical project management approaches and the real life situation. It turned out that there is a significant gap between theory and practice as not all theoretical concepts are transferable into practice. Therefore, the project management team had to realize these situations and find ways to realize solutions for that gap.

As a conclusion, this project was a win win situation for both the customer and the students since the faculty got a cheap solution for its business need and the students gained useful knowledge and experiences for their later career.

## REFERENCES

Balzert, H. (1998), „Lehrbuch der Software-Technik II", 1st Edition, Spektrum Akademischer Verlag, Wiesbaden.

Henrich, A. (2002), "Management von Softwareprojekten", 3rd Edition, Oldenburg.

Projektmanagement Blog (2007), „Work Breakdown Structure (WBS) / Projektstrukturplan", Online available at: http://www.pm-blog.de/2007/03/03/work-breakdown-structure-wbs-projektstrukturplan/, Called 24.09.2007

Steinweg, C. (2005), „Management der Softwareentwicklung, Projektkompass für die Erstellung von leistungsfähigen IT-Systemen", 6th Edition, Vieweg+Teubner, Wiesbaden

Zuser, W., Biffl, S., Grechenig, T. and Köhle, M. (2001), "Software Engineering mit UML und dem Unified Process", 2nd Edition, Pearson Studium, München.

# TEACHING TECHNOLOGY THROUGH IMMERSIVE PROJECTS: TRICKS OF THE TRADE

Fred L. Kitchens, Miller College of Business, Ball State University, Muncie, Indiana, USA, fkitchens@bsu.edu

## ABSTRACT

*Systems Analysis and Design is taught by the author in the college of business. It is a two-semester sequence of courses using the immersive learning style of teaching (aka: Service Learning), where a community partner from outside the university is the client. A team of students works with the client to provide a real business solution. This paper reviews the author's history and development of this teaching method and presents an outline of activities for the two-semester course following both the System Development Lifecycle and the Group Development model throughout the project.*

*Keywords: Immersive Learning, System Development Lifecycle, Group Development Model, Service Learning.*

## INTRODUCTION

The author's university promotes the use of "Immersive Learning" to provide students an opportunity not only to apply the knowledge and skills gained in the classroom; but also to gain insight to processes, learn from the academic disciplines of fellow teammates, and to develop the initiative to 'figure it out on their own' where necessary.

Closely related to "Experiential Learning," and "Service Learning," The term "Immersive Learning" pertains to a specific type of project-based experience in which students work directly with community partners outside the university. There are seven specific immersive criteria; most, preferably all, are required to qualify a project as "immersive":

1. A group of students, preferably interdisciplinary, working collaboratively
2. Work under the guidance of a faculty mentor
3. Students drive the learning process, determining the direction of the project

4. Students work with community partners
5. The experience produces a tangible outcome or product such as a business venture, DVD, or creative work that is a benefit to the community and to the students
6. Provides students with an industry connection
7. Students receive academic credit

The author has taught a two-semester sequence of courses in Systems Analysis and Design for eight years, and the Information Systems departmental capstone course for 3 years. In that time, he has mentored 23 free projects at two semesters each, 4 funded projects at two semesters each, and 6 competitive projects at one semester each. The author's methods, practice, and teaching theory have evolved over time. While his current process of teaching immersive learning has settled into a semi-stable, consistent model, it is still evolving, and growing in some subtle but important ways.

This paper reviews the author's current practices in teaching immersive learning projects in the information systems curriculum, and addresses some of the recent changes made to the course.

## BACKGROUND, DEVELOPMENT, AND LITERATURE REVIEW

The author's primary project-based course is Systems Analysis and Design in the Information Systems major curriculum of the college of business. Information Systems is not specifically 'hardware' and is not specifically 'software'; these subjects are taught in the Technology major and Computer Science major on the author's campus. Information Systems is the method – electronic or otherwise – used to collect, store, manipulate, and disseminate the information used to drive the processes that run an organization. Systems Analysis and Design is the process of analysing the processes to determine the system needs so that an appropriate system can be designed to transmit data and information for the organization. In short, Systems Analysis and Design is the application of hardware and software to solve business problems.

For the first couple of years the author tried to manage the student teams through the use of the System Development Lifecycle (SDLC), preached in almost every Systems Analysis and Design and Project Management textbook (Gido & Clements 2003; VanHorn, Schwarzkopf & Price, 2006; Dennis & Wixom, 2003). A simple curriculum consisting of the four basic SDLC stages - planning, analysis, design, and implementation - seemed a straight forward simple approach.

Over the course of the first couple of years it became readily obvious that the straight-forward approach to mentoring student projects with only the System Development Lifecycle as a guide was insufficient. Student teams were not functioning as expected. Otherwise straight forward projects were suffering due to team-dynamics. An attempt at solving the problem by bolstering the "planning" phase and strengthening specific tasks such as creating team standards, assigning roles, and defining objectives showed only moderate and short-term improvement for the beginning of the project. Another, more enduring approach was needed.

The Group Development model was applied to the projects by overlaying it on top of the System Development Lifecycle. While the SDLC provided a roadmap for the student teams, the Group Development model provided a way of understanding and managing the student teams (Tuchman, 1965). The first four stages of the model, Forming, Storming, Norming, and Performing, seemed to roughly correspond to the timing and sequence of the four steps in the SDLC model – or at least close enough for classroom purposes. The fifth stage, Adjourning, provided an enjoyable and educational way to wrap-up the academic year by recapping the students experiences and celebrating their accomplishments through an "Executive Retreat" where part of the departmental assessment data could also be gathered.

Eventually, it was determined that students needed more guidance than they were receiving from the textbook and lectures. They needed real examples of transformative Systems Analysis and Design projects. The book Reengineering the Corporation provided not only examples, but a roadmap to truly revolutionary system development (Hammer & Champy, 2001). The book encourages systems analysts to think outside the bubble, while focusing business processes and systemic solutions to business problems. It proved to be an excellent companion to the traditional Systems Analysis and Design textbook by bringing a big-picture and real-world perspective to the students' attention.

In previous years the author's university, like many universities, received feedback from alumni and the business community concerning their graduates' lack of effective business communication skills – both written and oral. The author addresses the written communication problem by changing to a new grading system. Changing from the traditional "90, 80, 70, 60" percent scale, the author adopted a scale representing an answer to the question, "If you (student) turned in a report of this quality to your manager a year from now (after you graduate), how embarrassed would I be if you told him that I taught you how to do this?" In answer to this question, the scores on graded papers are in a range of 0-100%, with the following stated implications behind the scores:

- 0% = don't even turn in a report of this low quality
- 25% = don't tell your manager where you went to school
- 50% = you may tell them that I taught you, but only if they ask first
- 75% = be sure to tell your manager that I taught you to write like this
- 100% = I would be honoured to be your co-author

As can be expected, the grading *scale* needed to be curved downward to meet the new scores. But, students seemed to appreciate the real-world, business comparison of their skills, and with proper coaching started showing dramatic improvement in their writing skills.

In response to the concern for oral business presentation skills, the book, *Reengineering the Corporation* by Michael Hammer and James Champy provided an opportunity to work on the students' presentation skills. The chapters in the book are divided equally among the 2 to 4 teams in class, each team receiving 4 to 7 opportunities to practice their presentation skills. The classroom presentations, with appropriate critical review by the author and by fellow classmates, provide a practice-ground for the major presentation at the end of the semester. At the end of the first semester, students have completed the Planning and Analysis stages of the SDLC. At the major presentation, student teams present their projects to a panel of alumni, as though they are bidding on the project. The alumni are instructed to make the students defend their position; and to make the presentation *the hardest presentation the students will ever have to make in their entire lives*. The goal is that every future presentation in their working careers should be easy in comparison.

## METHODS

The two-semester sequence of courses is designed with four objectives in mind:
1. Effectively teach Systems Analysis and Design
2. Provide a quality Immersive Experience that students can talk about when they interview
3. Refine written business communication skills
4. Improve oral business presentation skills

To accomplish these objectives, the following curriculum outline is followed:

### First Semester, First 3 weeks: Classroom organization and project initiation

During this time, the students are introduced and oriented to the project. Major tasks include submitting resumes so that at the end of this stage teams can be selected in a round-robin style "hiring" process conducted by student team leaders. Once the teams are selected, projects are assigned by the professor. This stage is not associated with any stage of Group Development, because the groups have generally not yet been formed.

During this time, lectures cover the planning procedures so that students know what to do once the teams are formed.

### First Semester, Weeks 4-6: Planning stage of SDLC and Forming stage of Group Development

Student teams go through a 3 week period in which they plan the project, including activities such as developing a GANTT chart, establishing team standards, and assigning roles for the project. This period is generally characterized by the Forming stage of group development.

During this time, teams begin to conduct presentations covering chapters in the book Reengineering the Corporation. Critiques of the presentations get progressively more difficult as skills improve.

## First Semester, Weeks 7-13: Analysis stage of SDLC and Storming stage of Group Development

The next 7 weeks of the first semester are devoted to the Analysis phase of the SDLC, and loosely equate to the Storming phase of the Group Development model.

Classroom presentations continue in this stage, eventually made more challenging and realistic by carefully-planned interruptions such as cell phones ringing, interruptions from outside the classroom, and distracting behaviour from certain audience members.

Student teams conduct the typical Analysis-stage activities such as information gathering, requirements determination, feasibility study, developing use-cases, data flow diagrams, and data modelling. The last task in this stage is to use the Multiple Criteria Decision Analysis technique to determine the future direction of the project (Belton & Stewart, 2002).

By the end of the phase most student teams have usually transitioned from Storming into the Norming stage of the Group Development model. A few teams seem to have a difficult time transitioning out of the Storming phase. The professor is better able to help teams transition when he understands the phases and their characteristics.

## First Semester, Weeks 14-15: No-Man's Land

The last two weeks of the first semester are reserved for preparing a major presentation for the alumni judges. Students present their projects as though they are bidding on the project. This means they have to revise their earlier project planning expectations to show that they know how to complete the project, they have to estimate the cost for completion, and they have to prepare a sales presentation for the alumni judges.

Alumni judges consist of departmental Advisory Board members and alumni from past classes. They are instructed to make the presentation the hardest presentation the students will ever have in their lives – past and future – so that every future presentation is comparatively easy. A debriefing is held immediately after the presentation, as well as a broader debriefing during the last class meeting of the semester to review and reflect upon the presentation experience.

## Second Semester, Weeks 1-7: Design phase of SDLC and Norming phase of Group Development

In the second semester, the students proceed with the project as though they received the contract to complete the work described in their major presentation proposal. This usually requires some revisions to be made first, based on feedback from the alumni judges. Seven weeks are allotted to this because the teams generally have to research all of the available alternatives, narrow down the feasible solutions, and evaluate them using the Multiple Criteria Decision Analysis method. Depending on the project, the difficult part is sometimes developing the technology plan to make everything work.

While the Norming phase has hopefully already begun, this phase is generally associated with the Norming stage of Group development. Some groups never get past the Norming phase; they get stuck in this phase throughout the duration of the semester.

## Second Semester, Weeks 8-10: Implementation phase of SDLC and Performing phase of Group Development

In this stage, teams are instructed to develop an implementation plan that is so detailed; the client could (for example) hand their completed plan to a summer intern and reasonably expect it to be completed properly. At the end of this phase, the students make a final presentation to the client. Presentations are made in a corporate board room when one is available. Forty percent of the students' grade is based on the final report and presentation. But, before it will be graded, the client must accept it – meaning that if it is not accepted by the client, the grade is a 'zero' for forty percent of the course.

Hopefully, by this point the student teams are in the Performing stage of Group Development. Unfortunately, very few teams in real life ever get to this stage. In a somewhat controlled classroom environment, it is to some extent easier for the professor to help the teams achieve the Performing stage. It is important to try because once a student has experienced that stage, it will be easier for them to recognize it and help future work-teams get there.

## Second Semester, Weeks 11-15: Completed SDLC and Adjourning phase of Group Development

In the aftermath of a major two-semester immersive project, two important things take place; a Senior Class Executive Retreat, and an opportunity to review and practice their new-found skills and experience.

The Senior Class Executive Retreat is conducted on a Saturday, late in the second semester. Students are taken to an off-campus location, away from the distractions of campus, for a 4-5 hour retreat. The retreat begins with a keynote speaker who leads a discussion about the transition from college to business, and the process of managing one's own career. This is followed by some type of group sporting or recreational activity, as in most business retreats. Lunch is provided by the department, and includes an awards ceremony where students are recognized for everything from top student in each senior class, to peer-recognition awards from most respected, most improved, etc... Finally, students are lead through a brainstorming activity using the Nominal Group Technique to determine the "Top 10 things the department or the college can improve for future students."

The Nominal Group Technique process is used with three goals in mind: First, to flush out any ideas for improvement for the department, and for the project experience. Second, it is used to encourage students to reflect upon what they gained from the project experience. Third, it starts the process of encouraging students to think like loyal, active alumni. In fact, several alumni usually show up to participate in the Executive Retreat every year.

Following the retreat, students are presented with a competition in which they are able to compete for cash awards against their fellow peers from other classes, using the skills they gained in the immersive project experience. A nearby national headquarters for a large chain of restaurants sponsors a competition consisting of a mini-version of the larger systems analysis and design project. This does three things: First, it gives students an opportunity to practice the skills they learned. Second, if gives students an opportunity to realize just how much they really did learn. Third, if a team has not yet broken into the Performing stage of Group Development, they often will get there in this activity. Changing tasks, and competing against teams from other courses, who they know to be less experienced often helps.

## CONCLUSIONS

The course curriculum outlined is difficult and time consuming, for both the students and the professor. But, it is also very rewarding for both.

All four of the initial objectives are met:

1. Effectively teach Systems Analysis and Design: the largest percentage of students from this course pursue a career in IS or IT Consulting.
2. Provide a quality immersive experience that students can talk about when they interview: Almost every student reports that the project is the number one thing the employers wanted to talk about in their interviews. Often they are told that they were hired because of their project experience.
3. Refine written business communication skills: alumni often ask for the professor's project outline to use in their jobs. Some have been rewarded with jobs or promotions for the writing skills learned in this course.
4. Improve oral business presentation skills: alumni of this program often report that in future business presentations, they were the only presenter who was calm, cool, and collected.

In the past two years, every graduating senior from this sequence of courses has had a job offer before graduation. The alumni of this program tend to be more loyal and more supportive than other alumni.

# REFERENCES

Belton, V., & Stewart, T. J. (2002). Multiple Criterion Decision Analysis: An Integrated Approach, Kluwer Academic Publishers, Boston.

Dennis, A. & Wixon, B.H. (2003), "Systems Analysis and Design; an Applied Approach", 2$^{nd}$ Edition, John Wiley & Sons, Inc., USA.

Gido, J. & Clements, J.P. (2003), "Successful Project management," 2$^{nd}$ Edition, Thomson Learning, USA.

Gora, J.A., "President Gora's fall 2006 faculty/staff convocation remarks" Emens Auditorium, 8/18/2006, www.bsu.edu.

Hammer, M., Champy, J. (2001), "Reengineering the Corporation; a Manifesto for Business Revolution," HarperCollins Publishers, USA.

Tuckman, Bruce. (1965), "Developmental sequence in small groups," Psychological bulletin, 63, 384-399.

VanHorn, R.L., Schwarzkopf, A.B., & Price, R.L. (2006), "Information Systems Solutions; A Project Approach", McGraw-Hill Irwin, New York, NY.

# IT RISK MANAGEMENT AT SUPIDO

Lorenz Hartmann, University of Mannheim. lorenz.hartmann@web.de. ++49 176 23531591

Boris Toma, University of Mannheim. boristoma@gmx.de. ++49 163 2650027

Christopher Zygor, University of Mannheim. czygor@hotmail.com. ++49 176 23732840

Supervisor: Prof. Dr. Armin Heinzl, University of Mannheim. heinzl@uni-mannheim.de

## INTRODUCTION

One evening in September 2007 Yukiu Shikibu, CEO of Supido Europe Inc. was pondering about risk. He asked himself how it was possible that until now he has never really taken IT risks into account before. Personally, he was very well insured, in fact he was insured against all kinds of dangers. In Japan, he even signed a flood-insurance although he lived several miles away from the coast.

In terms of Supido Europe he was mainly thinking about business risks to make sure that the company was protected whenever needed. But IT risks? Shikibu was aware of the fact that every IT department was under a certain risk and that no IT system could be totally out of errors. But lowering or even avoiding IT risk was an option he had never given a thought before. It was not rocket science for sure, but somehow it had not occurred to him. Now he was facing a decision that would guide the direction of Supido Europe´s IT for the future.

The key question was: Who of his board members had the most suitable recommendation? Was it Hideki Nagashima, his old friend from Japan who already worked together with him in Sapporo? Or Edgar Gentenaar who had the most experience and was responsible for the numbers he reports to the headquarters in Japan? Or was it Markus Stemmer, his young German CIO who probably had the most IT knowledge?

Shikibu knew that everybody had his own stakes in this game, but he had to see through these personal affairs and do the best for Supido….

# SUPIDO

## Historical background

Supido was founded in 1880 by Hiroshi Yoshiba near Sapporo in Japan. Originally Supido was a producer of steam engines with no connection to the automotive industry. In 1921, three years after taking over the company from his father, Akira Yoshiba decided to start with the production of vehicles, although there were already several competitors in the market. His vision was to use Supido´s existing production plants in order to produce luxury cars which offered an amount of customization nobody else did. This remained Supido´s business maxim until today. In 1953, Supido changed its name to Supido Motors Corporation along with the initial public offer.

Ten years later, in 1963, the first car was exported to Germany. For the first time, Supido cars were exported to Europe by local importers. Prior to this, the only country Supido cars were exported to was the USA. It took Supido five more years to realize the potential of the European, especially the German market, when Supido´s management decided to build the first European sales unit in Germany in order to market cars on their own. Nevertheless, it was Rotterdam where Supido wanted to establish the European headquarters in 1973. At first Germany was preferred since it was the biggest European division and the IT was already placed there, but some other reasons finally tipped the balance for Rotterdam:

First, Rotterdam with its harbor provided a better shipping connection to Japan than Essen did and second, the Dutch taxation laws promised higher profits. Furthermore, Germany was not considered politically stable enough by some board members. Nowadays, Supido is the number two in selling Japanese luxury class cars behind Toyota with its luxury vehicle division Lexus. It has one division on each continent and is selling cars in all over the world. Although Supido is represented internationally, production solely remained in Sapporo.

## Supido Europe today

After the home market in Asia and the North American market, Europe is the market where Supido sells the third most cars and where the highest growth potential is being seen. Today Supido Europe employs around 1,200 people in several administrational, logistical and sales functions. About 28,000 cars are sold in Europe; Germany with its 5,000 cars is the market with the highest demand. This makes Supido number four in the segment regarding sales in Europe behind Mercedes, BMW and Audi.

These sales mount up to a total turnover of more than 1.1 billion Euros resulting in an EBIT of almost 100 million Euros. Supido Europe has to "buy" the cars in Japan at the price of net costs, so the added value is only reached through the marketing and distribution in Europe. The logistics centre itself "sells" the cars almost at market price, so that the whole profit is made at the logistics centre in Rotterdam.

## MARKET CHARACTERISTICS AND STRATEGY

Over the years, Supido gained more and more market share in the segment of luxury cars. It is a tough market with a high competition level but also promises high margins. A constant drive for innovation, high quality and high service levels are crucial factors. Surveys show, that the most important criteria for buying a car in Europe are the following (order by importance):

- Reliability
- Safety
- Comfort
- Price-performance ratio
- Overall cost
- Environmental friendliness

Therefore Supido's business strategy focus is less on costs, but rather on quality and individuality. Another important aspect in Supido´s strategy is to assure short delivery times and a good logistical supply. Evidence for the important role of logistics is the establishment of an own logistics centre. Environmental consciousness is the criteria which gained most weight in the last years. Still it is uncertain whether this is just a notion of today or a longer lasting trend and how it affects the market of luxury cars.

Nevertheless, the combination of luxury and environmental consciousness is considered as a strategic advantage by Supido. Like most Japanese automotive producers Supido has a good reputation regarding environmental consciousness. In this domain, but also in other areas like comfort, Supido aims at being an innovation leader and introduces continuously new models and spare parts. In order to succeed with this strategy, Supido requires a flexible and reliable supply system.

## SUPIDO EUROPE´S ORGANIZATION

### Management strategy

Generally Supido Europe´s management is strongly influenced by the Japanese central. In the entire corporation Supido put a main focus on loyalty, both internally (regarding employees) and externally (regarding suppliers and customers). Consensus on decisions was another important aspect in Supido´s management philosophy, as well as the picture of collective success and failure.

For a long time, the implementation of this philosophy was a big problem in Europe. Most top management positions were fulfilled by European managers, who did not see the necessity of the whole loyalty concept and disregarded it. Communication within top management hardly existed, most board meetings ended open with the CEO deciding on his own in the end. After some attempts to change this management behavior, the board in Japan decided to stop tolerating this management style in 2002. Due to that many top managers had to leave. The idea was to implement a younger top management that was willing to communicate and follow orders, even at cost of lack of experience.

### Supido headquarters Europe, Rotterdam

As already mentioned, Supido Europe´s headquarters is located in Rotterdam including administration, accounting and top management (**Exhibit 1** shows full organizational chart).

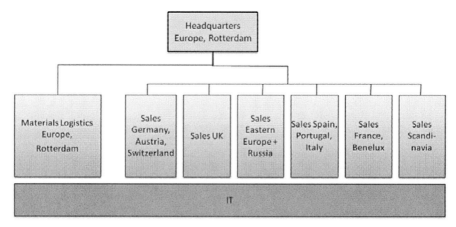

***Exhibit 1*** *Organizational Chart of Supido Europe (Source: Supido)*

CEO of Supido Europe is Yukibu Shikibu. After feeling to lose control over the European subsidiary with the last Dutch CEO in 2002, the board decided to place a trusted Japanese in the CEO position. The choice fell upon Shikibu, who had become executive vice president in Japan just the year before. He was considered the best option to gain more control over Supido Europe again because he was young, modern thinking, ambitious and at the same time loyal. When Shikibu arrived in Rotterdam, he was welcomed by Edgar Gentenaar. Gentenaar worked since the foundation of Supido Europe in the headquarters in Rotterdam after graduating from the local university. For 15 years now, he was holding the CFO position. He was brilliant with numbers and always kept a tight eye on every investment. Sometimes too tight, critics said…

Right next to the headquarters Supido Europe´s logistics centre can be found. In the beginning, logistics was treated like a normal business function of the headquarters such as accounting or finance. But after some time, the department grew and became more and more a key function as cars and spare parts needed to be shipped to Europe. So top management decided to spin off the logistics department into an own logistics centre next door with an own chief, the Head of Logistics.

Head of Logistics was Thomas Hauke from Hamburg. He worked for a big German logistics company until he got an offer from Supido in 2004. There he was especially responsible for the shipping department. He was always content with his job in Hamburg, but the challenge to be responsible for such a big department was attracting him.

## Supido organization and sales division, Germany

As already mentioned, in Essen / Germany the first department of Supido in Europe was built up. During that time, some kind of top management was established. Parts of it remained in the position of the Chief Organizational Officer in Germany. He is responsible for organizational issues in Europe and the IT. The IT department is still centralized in Germany. In the beginning, this was just for cost reasons because it seemed too expensive and was considered unnecessary since IT was not considered really a management function back then. Nowadays, although the strategic potential of IT was realized, nobody dared to touch the IT department. The COO position is fulfilled by Hideki Nagashima. He came along with Shikibu in 2003. They were close friends and went to college together. In Japan, Nagashima worked as Shikibu´s assistant. In Europe he saw his chance to step up to the front row as a member of the board.

Below him, as CIO, a young German named Markus Stemmer is responsible for the centralized IT department. He formerly worked five years at ITTT as a software consultant, when he got an offer during a consulting project by Supido. Furthermore, Supido had sales divisions in each European region with sales managers who were all reporting to Nagashima (**Exhibit 2** shows hierarchy structure).

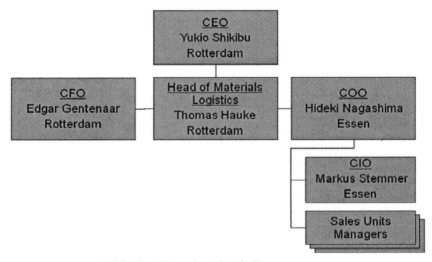

***Exhibit 2*** *Hierarchy at Supido Europe (Source: Supido)*

# A SPECIAL RELATIONSHIP

## From CTO to CIO

From an outside view, business operations seemed to work quite well at Supido. But under the surface there were murmurs in the company. Especially the relationship between Hideki Nagashima and the ambitious CIO Stemmer was very tense. It was the way he got the job and the way top management acted what made Nagashima still furious.

In January 2004 the former CTO Adam Richter announced to retire in the upcoming summer. So there was a critical need for a new head of IT. Primarily Nagashima should take over the lead of the IT department and integrate it into his area of competencies. But CEO Shikibu was not sure about that, because he wanted to transfer the IT department from a technical unit like it was to a more strategic, customer related unit which was more flexible to the need of the business. Although Nagashima was a friend of him, Shikibu asked himself the question, if it would be possible for Nagashima to focus enough on this task and to be successful in it.

The solution for this problem came by chance. During an ITTT consulting project at Supido, Shikibu met Markus Stemmer. The way how Stemmer led the project was impressive. Shikibu got the impression that he did not just put out some blueprints, but rather put effort in it and really understood the business. In a face-to-face talk, Shikibu got to know that Stemmer was not very happy with his situation at ITTT and was searching for a new challenge. From that point on things developed quickly. Stemmer joined the company just one month after this meeting with the CEO in order to familiarize himself with the new duty. Three months later he became new head of IT, which was called CIO from that time on. Trying not to alienate Nagashima, Shikibu abolished the plan to liftthe CIO position on top management level, and stuck to the old hierarchy with the CIO just reporting to the COO.

## An internal conflict

But this decision should bring much trouble along. Nagashima never understood the appointment of Stemmer and tried to throw obstacles in Stemmer's path wherever possible, but not too obviously. It was bad luck for him, that Stemmer was a smart guy who knew this kind of game from his time at ITTT. From day one Stemmer was totally convinced to establish his ideas and break with IT history. He was a real visionary, always looking for the great hit and was not too much interested in the small tasks of daily life. Due to the reorganization of the IT department (**Exhibit 3** shows IT Organization), he introduced a new customer related mentality and tried to homogenize IT infrastructure. In most cases he had to reduce the speed of change and be cautious because Nagashima tried to find possibilities to discredit his work at top-management meetings. Shikibu had the feeling hat there might be an internal conflict between Stemmer and Nagashima, but he was not sure about that. Stemmer never lost a bad word about Nagashima. If he did so because of fairness or because of loyalty, Shikibu did not know.

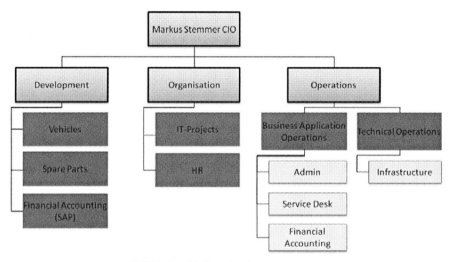

***Exhibit 3***    *IT Organization (Source: Supido)*

Even there was a strong need for communication, the lack of collegiality between Nagashima and Stemmer led to a mentality of silence. In processes which were related to operations and IT the responsibilities were not clearly clarified. Nagashima knew of that, but he saw the possibility to discredit Stemmer if an error would occur. So he did not advise him to put more emphasis on this topic.

## THE "WAKE UP CALL"

### A harmful incident

The incident happened on the 10th of August. Nagashima got a phone call from Japan early in the morning. At the other end of the line was Masahiko Funaki, COO of Supido Motors Corporation, Japan. Although the situation was really critical, he was polite as always. "Good morning Mr. Nagashima, I am sorry that I have to wake you up so early in the morning but I think we have a serious problem!" Nagashima was awake right away and in fact, what Funaki told him was a real problem. Three hours earlier an irregularity occurred in the section of detailed planning in production. An employee detected that there were 60 cars scheduled identically like the day before. The order was immediately changed to "hold on" and other orders were prioritized. Nevertheless the problem was detected very late. Due to the "just-in-time" principle of production at Supido, orders were already sent out. To fix the problem, they would have to spend much effort and of course money on the issue. "It is too early to know what went wrong", Funakai said, "but I think we got the same order from Europe twice." Funaki was right. Four days ago there was a double booking in the system. The overall operational loss was estimated 145.000 €. Nagashima was struggling. It would jeopardize his position in the company if it was his fault, but because the SAP Accounting system was affected, he might pass the buck to Stemmer.

Having his back up against the wall, Nagashima set in a team to find out what exactly happened. After two weeks the team reported to him. On the 6th of August an employee in the head office of Supido Europe tried to transmit all vehicle orders from the week before via SAP Accounting to Japan, which was weekly routine. But on this day, the responsible employee was not able to forward the orders to Japan. Because of that the employee called the Service Desk, which could not help because the problem never occurred before. They tried to solve the problem by asking the technical operations. The person there was not surprised. There was a software change on the server the day before, made by the development. This change was not communicated to the users. He sent a request to the development of SAP Accounting. The employee there forwarded the orders manually to fix the problem, which resulted in the two identical orders sent to Japan.

**Shikibu's reaction**

When Shikibu got the report he was really angry, but tried to calm down and think about the situation. His impression was that it was the fault of both: Stemmer, because he was too much into strategy and not that much into operations; Nagashima because he did not comply with the task to control what the CIO was doing. Thousands of questions were in his head: "Why does the Service level support not know about the server change? Are there any communication processes existing? Why is the developer able to make changes on the business environment?" But the main question was: "Why the hell do I have to think about issues Nagashima and Stemmer are responsible for?" Shikibu got the feelings that there was the need for a neutral person to bring things back to balance. He had read about a leading provider of risk consulting called Protiviti, which was operating in the field of IT risk. "Protiviti might be a good solution", he thought, stood up from his chair walked to the window and looked out on Rotterdam harbor.

When Nagashima and Stemmer heard of it, they realized that Shikibu lost trust in them. Especially Stemmer was annoyed losing his clean slate. He phoned Shikibu telling him that he carried the whole responsibility for the incident but that he had learned his lesson and would focus more on risks in the future. But Shikibu did not change his decision. In his eyes the error was to harmful. He had to know if things like that could happen again. The incident had shown that Stemmer might need external consultancy. So Shikibu assigned Stemmer to contact Protiviti to present their company.

A week later Mitch Spencer, manager and automotive expert, and Chris Miller, Senior Consultant, introduced Protiviti and its company profile to the board. When they heard what happened at Supido the consultants recommended to first of all conduct a Risk Assessment at the IT. So they could get an overview of the IT and report inherent risks to the board. That was exactly what Shikibu was looking for.

## PROTIVITI

Protiviti is a wholly owned subsidiary of Robert Half International Inc., a $4.0 billion public firm listed on the New York Stock Exchange (NYSE symbol: RHI). Founded in 1948, Robert Half International is the world's first and largest specialized staffing firm. The company places professionals on a project and full-time basis in the fields of accounting and finance, technology, office administration, legal support, and creative services.

Protiviti is a leading provider of independent risk consulting and internal audit services. They provide consulting and advisory services to help clients identify, assess, measure and manage financial, operational and technology-related risks encountered in their industries, and assist in the implementation of the processes and controls to enable their continued monitoring. Protiviti employs more than 2.900 professionals at 60 offices worldwide. Their clients include more than 35 percent of all Fortune 100 companies and more than 25 percent of all Fortune 500 companies.

In Germany Protiviti is sub-divided into three divisions: Business Risk, Technology Risk and Internal Audit. Business Risk identifies, prioritizes, and manages risks to enhance performance and ultimately, business value. Technology Risk comprises IT Governance based on five Competence Areas: Strategy & Organization, Value & Performance, Risk & Security, Control & Monitoring and Audit & Compliance. At last Internal Audit offers a full spectrum of value-creating services, technologies, and skills for management, directors, and the internal audit community.

# ASSESSING IT RISKS

### The initial phase

When CIO Markus Stemmer met Mitch Spencer from Protiviti the first time, he told him what had happened on that awful day at Supido. Stemmer still could not believe what happened to his IT. So much the better it was that he had called experts to analyze his IT now. Spencer had some years consulting experience in the automotive industry and brought along Chris Miller, leader of Protiviti's Competence Area "Risk & Security" and expert regarding Risk Assessments. As Supido had never really cared about risks in IT and neither had a risk management nor a control framework implemented, Protiviti had advised the board to do a Risk Assessment, an identification and evaluation of potential IT risks.

Spencer and Miller started with a workshop on Supido's IT together with Stemmer, the application managers and some users from the business. The consultants primarily wanted to get an overview of Supido's IT resources. This included the IT systems, components, staff and processes. Stemmer and his colleagues could provide Protiviti with information about IT staff, but they noticed their documentation of processes, systems and components was incomplete. Therefore Stemmer commissioned the application managers to work on an IT landscape. Some days went by when the desired documents were forwarded to the CIO, Spencer and Miller.

## IT landscape of Supido

The IT at Supido was based on three main systems. The core element was the SAP system, which offered internal and external accounting and all kind of ERP-functions for logistics. Besides SAP there were two more systems, named "Vehicles" and "Spare Parts". They were kind of similar. On the one side they were providing information like prices, delivery times, availability of goods and specialties; on the other side they forwarded sales information to the SAP system. Although there were some differences between the systems, they were generally homogeneous. On the front end side there were several different application systems in the sales clusters. Key application was the car configurator which Stemmer introduced in 2005. According to the customer oriented strategy of Supido, it gave customers the possibility to create their own individual car.

## Self-assessment

Protiviti's consultants announced the importance of the IT landscape in regard to the identification of inherent IT risks (**Exhibit 4** shows Protiviti's IT Risk Model; Risk Assessment covers the first three steps).

**Exhibit 4**     *Protiviti IT Risk Model (Source: Protivi)*

Chris Miller continued by doing some interviews with Stemmer and his application managers based on a self-assessment. Using the IT landscape, first they had to rate applications and infrastructure regarding the Application risk (e.g. integrity, sensitivity etc.) and the impact on business risk factors (e.g. operational, financial reporting etc.). Besides applications they had to define whether processes are centralized, managed by application or not managed. These processes then had to be assessed by their risk (reliability & efficiency, consistency etc.) and their impact on business factors. This evaluation was hard work for Stemmer and his staff, but they were highly supported by Protiviti's consultants. They always posed the correct questions at the right time. Stemmer was really happy about having external expertise at this project.

## The evaluation process

After Mitch Spencer and Chris Miller got the interviews and let some users fill out questionnaires they had a list of possible IT threats. Markus Stemmer became silent when he saw that list. But Spencer calmed him down and noticed that this was not the result of their risk assessment. "Now we have a list of inherent risks. But we do not know to what extent they are imperiling." he said.

Stemmer was not sure about how risks could be quantified, when Chris Miller told him that Protiviti had developed a Risk Evaluation Tool based on qualitative methods. As in commerce and industry there were barely loss databases such as in the financial services industry the use of quantitative methods was not possible. But in this way risks could be rated and prioritized as well.

Chris Miller collected all the data carried out in the self-assessment and inputted it into the risk tool (**Exhibit 5 and 6** show Risk Tool input variables from the process and application view). The tool evaluated applications, infrastructure and processes and outputted a risk matrix quoting overall application risk and process risk according to priority.

| II (B) Risk Rating for IT Processes | | | | | | | | | | |
|---|---|---|---|---|---|---|---|---|---|---|
| *Jump to Risk Bank Criteria Definitions* | | | | | | | | | | |
| Process Information | | | RISK of Achieving IT Process Criteria | | | | | | Impact of Application on | |
| IT Process | Management Structure | Process Weight | Reliability & Efficiency | Consistency | Technology Leverage | Results Management | Human Capital | Complexity | Strategic | Operational |
| 4.1 Define IT Strategy and Organization | By Application | 100% | #NAME? | #NAME? | #NAME? | #NAME? | #NAME? | #NAME? | #NAME? | #NAME? |
| 4.1.1 Develop and Maintain the IT Strategy | By Application | 33.3% | Medium | Medium | High | High | Low | High | High | Low |
| 4.1.2 Define and Manage the IT Organization | By Application | 33.3% | Low | Medium | High | High | Low | High | High | High |
| 4.1.3 Develop and Maintain the IT Governance Structure | Non Managed | 33.3% | Medium | Medium | High | Medium | Medium | High | High | High |
| 4.2 Manage Security and Privacy | Non Managed | 100% | #NAME? | #NAME? | #NAME? | #NAME? | #NAME? | #NAME? | #NAME? | #NAME? |
| 4.2.1 Security / Privacy Strategy and Communication | Non Managed | 15.0% | Medium | Medium | High | High | Medium | Medium | Low | Medium |
| 4.2.2 Administer Security (Add, Change, Delete Users) | Non Managed | 35.0% | Medium | Medium | High | High | Medium | Medium | Low | High |
| 4.2.3 Manage Security Incidents | Non Managed | 30.0% | High | High | High | High | High | High | Medium | High |
| 4.2.4 Monitor Regulatory Compliance | Centralized | 20.0% | Medium | Medium | Medium | High | Low | High | High | Low |
| 4.3 Deploy and Maintain Solutions | Non Managed | 100% | #NAME? | #NAME? | #NAME? | #NAME? | #NAME? | #NAME? | #NAME? | #NAME? |
| 4.3.1 Manage Systems Development Life Cycle | By Application | 40.0% | Medium | High | High | Medium | Low | Medium | High | Low |
| 4.3.2 Develop and Maintain Application Interfaces | Non Managed | 20.0% | Medium | Medium | High | High | Low | High | Low | Medium |
| 4.3.3 Manage Application Changes | Non Managed | 40.0% | High | High | High | High | Medium | High | Low | High |
| 4.4 Support End Users | Non Managed | 100% | #NAME? | #NAME? | #NAME? | #NAME? | #NAME? | #NAME? | #NAME? | #NAME? |
| 4.4.1 Manage Incidents | Non Managed | 50.0% | High | High | High | High | Medium | Medium | Low | Medium |
| 4.4.2 Manage Problems | Non Managed | 25.0% | High | Medium | Medium | High | Medium | High | Low | High |
| 4.4.3 Manage Service | Centralized | 25.0% | Low | Low | Medium | Medium | Low | Low | Low | Medium |

**Exhibit 5**   *Risk Tool input variables – Process view (Source: Protivi)*

| II (A) Risk Rating for Critical Applications | | | | | | | |
|---|---|---|---|---|---|---|---|
| *Jump to Risk Bank Criteria Definitions* | | | | | | | |
| Application Information | | | Impact of Application on Business Risk Factors | | | | |
| Business Unit | Application Name | Description | Financial Exposure | Strategic | Operational | Legal/Regulatory Compliance | Financial Reporting |
| Infrastructure Components | | | | | | | |
| All | MS Active Directory | User Management | High | Medium | High | Low | High |
| All | MQSeries | E-mail | High | Low | Medium | High | Medium |
| All | Cisco VPN | Security | Low | Low | High | Low | Low |
| Application Components | | | | | | | |
| | SAP Accounting | ERP, Internal/External Account | High | Medium | High | Medium | High |
| | Vehicles | Pricing, Delivery times, Availability, Combination possibilities | High | Medium | Medium | Low | Medium |
| | Spare Parts | Pricing, Delivery times, Availability | Medium | Low | Low | Medium | Medium |
| | | | High | Low | Medium | Medium | Low |

**Exhibit 6**     *Risk Tool input variables – Application view (Source: Supido)*

When Markus Stemmer perceived that result, he almost passed out. He could not believe his IT was that susceptible for risks. "What will Shikibu and Nagashima say?" he asked himself. His CEO and COO would believe a complete idiot of him, he thought. But Spencer and Miller from Protiviti laid him to rest. "That's not unusual for the first risk assessment" Chris Miller said. "If you see it from a different angle you have to be pleased that you are aware of risks now and that you can work on them." Spencer said. "It's all very well to say that." thought Markus Stemmer, only thinking about how to tell that to his CEO and COO. Nagashima had already asked for the results some days ago. It came to Stemmer that Nagashima is just waiting to see the findings to attack him again.

## THE BOTTOM LINE

### Results

Then the time had come and Spencer and Miller from Protiviti presented the risk assessment outcome to the board. Shikibu was very interested in the findings as well as his COO and CFO. Stemmer already knew what would come next. As it was obvious, Spencer told that there were vulnerable applications and processes at Supido's IT (**Exhibit 7** shows Risk Assessment findings). Especially the Active Directory was at risk regarding the management of security, the deployment and maintenance of solutions and the support of end users. Furthermore Supido's SAP accounting system was threatened. Developers were having access to the production environment which was the reason why cars were ordered twice. In addition there was no incident and change management process defined, so that the server was changed without testing and the user couldn't forward the orders to Japan. "All that merged on August 10th at your IT" Miller noticed. "It's time to be awake to IT risks and beyond to handle them" he said. Stemmer noticed that Shikibu pricked his ears at that moment. Nagashima unlike gave him a self-satisfied glance as if he was pleased about what had happened.

**III (A)  Select Application / Process Audit Areas**

| IT Process Area | Overall Risk Ranking → | Spare Parts | MS Active Directory | MQSeries | SAP Accounting | Vehicles | Cisco VPN |
|---|---|---|---|---|---|---|---|
| | | Low | High | Medium | High | Medium | Low |
| 4.1 Define IT Strategy and Organization | Medium | | | | | | |
| 4.1.1 Develop and Maintain the IT Strategy | Medium | | | | | | |
| 4.1.2 Define and Manage the IT Organization | Medium | | | | | | |
| 4.1.3 Develop and Maintain the IT Governance Structure | Medium | | | | | | |
| 4.2 Manage Security and Privacy | High | | | | | | |
| 4.2.1 Security / Privacy Strategy and Communication | Medium | | | | | | |
| 4.2.2 Administer Security (Add, Change, Delete Users) | High | | | | | | |
| 4.2.3 Manage Security Incidents | High | | | | | | |
| 4.2.4 Monitor Regulatory Compliance | Medium | | | | | | |
| 4.3 Deploy and Maintain Solutions | High | | | | | | |
| 4.3.1 Manage Systems Development Life Cycle | Medium | | | | | | |
| 4.3.2 Develop and Maintain Application Interfaces | High | | | | | | |
| 4.3.3 Manage Application Changes | High | | | | | | |
| 4.6 Support End Users | Medium | | | | | | |
| 4.6.1 Manage Incidents | High | | | | | | |
| 4.6.2 Manage Problems | High | | | | | | |
| 4.6.3 Manage Service | Low | | | | | | |

***Exhibit 7*** *Risk Assessment Results (Source: Protivi)*

Shikibu now asked Protiviti to make a proposal. Mitch Spencer then recommended to primarily work on the acute risk areas. This would include the definition and implementation of roles and responsibilities as well as the definition of an incident and change management process in a full-time project with two consultants. The project would add up to about 60.000 €.

In addition to that Spencer advised to establish risk management as an ongoing process within Supido's IT. If so Protiviti could give them two options. Within the first option Protiviti would occupy the project lead and train two FTE's from Supido so that within a year they would be able to handle risk management on their own. Spencer assumed a part-time project with a duration of about a year and project costs of about 110.000 €. The second option would include a project with only external resources. Protiviti would be responsible for Supido's IT risk management and provide a full-time consultant. The annual cost would amount 220.000 €. After Spencer had presented the facts Shikibu now had an overview of possible options. He appointed a meeting with Gentenaar, Nagashima and Stemmer and asked them for their thinking.

## The challenge

Gentenaar, still seeing IT as a cost factor, appreciated the presentation but it did not change his position at all. As CFO he would neither fix the acute problems nor install a risk management process. In his eyes that incident was part of operational risk. The loss of 145.000 € could be carried in regard to the project costs as incidents like that were happening approximately every five years.

In contrary to that Nagashima preferred the idea to work on the acute problems as well as to establish risk management as a recurring process. In his opinion Stemmer had already messed things up. Therefore he recommended to fully outsource risk management to Protiviti.

Finally Stemmer revealed his opinion to his CEO. He had recognized that his IT was vulnerable and there was no expertise in that area. That is why he would agree with Protiviti to fix the acute problems. Moreover he realized that risk management is an ongoing process. He suggested deploying a risk management division under the lead of Protiviti in the first year. Supido would profit from knowledge transfer and could provide the service on their own at the beginning of 2009.

Now Shikibu had enough information. It was time for a decision…

# ENABLING SOCIAL CONNECTEDNESS IN E-LEARNING

Ioana Ghergulescu, Computer and Software Engineering Department, University "Politehnica", Faculty of Automation and Computers, 2 Parvan, Timisoara, Romania, ioanag@ms.upt.ro,

Sabine Moebs, Performance Engineering Laboratory, RINCE, School of Electronic Engineering, Dublin City University, Dublin, Ireland, sabine@eeng.dcu.ie,

Jenifer McManis, Performance Engineering Laboratory, RINCE, School of Electronic Engineering, Dublin City University, Dublin, Ireland, mcmanisj@eeng.dcu.ie,

## ABSTRACT

*In the Internet age learning and communication have arrived at a different level. E-learning now uses intelligent tutor system and applies adaptive hypermedia systems. It does not support social connectedness by allowing communication with other learners. This can lead to feelings of isolation amongst learners and ultimately learner demotivation. This paper presents* **Connect!** *– a stand alone component for adaptive learning system to enable social connectedness in e-learning.*

*Keywords: Adaptive Hypermedia System, Social Connectedness, Web 2.0.*

## INTRODCUTION

Twenty-three million small and medium sized enterprises (SMEs) provide around 75 million jobs, that is two thirds of all jobs and 99% of all enterprises in Europe, states the Observatory of European SMEs. SMEs tend to maintain their staff even during economically difficult times, which makes them an important, stabilizing pillar of the national economies. The increasing globalization and the consequent competitiveness together with changing legal requirements force SMEs to permanently build up knowledge beyond their core area of expertise.

Successful learning is therefore crucial for small and medium sized enterprises (SMEs) for the achievement of knowledge and improving their position in market.[7]

The following research was done as part of a summer school at the Performance Engineering Lab in the School of Electronic Engineering at Dublin City

University. The project is embedded in ongoing research in the area of adaptive e-learning systems and aims to contribute a small piece to the work in the group.

## ADAPTIVE HYPERMEDIA SYSTEMS

Adaptive Hypermedia System is a new generation of hypermedia systems started in 1990s bringing together the two area: hypermedia and user modeling. Hypermedia is an extension to the term hypertext in which graphics, audio, text and hyperlinks create a generally non-linear medium of information. Bringing the user model to hypermedia, the non linear medium of information is changing after the user preferences for a device, after their goals, knowledge [1,2].

With adaptive hypermedia systems we refer to all hypertext and hypermedia systems which have information on the user, stored in the user model. These systems apply this model to adapt aspects of the system to the user. The 3 main features for an adaptive hypermedia system are characterized as a hypertext and hypermedia system, to include a user model as well as the ability to adapt the content to the user model[3] .

Adaptive Hypermedia systems for e-learning have in their architecture a user model, a domain model and an adaptation model (figure 1).

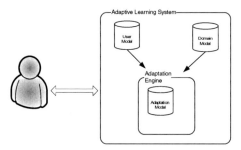

*Figure 1 Basic Architecture ALS [3]*

The user model represents characteristics of the user, their goals, their knowledge, their device preferences. The domain model represents the concepts of the subject domain and it describes these concept structures as concept maps, semantic networks or concept graphs. The adaptation model connects the two previously outlined models and any models relevant for the adaptation to the user's needs, using adaptation rules. It thus enables individualized selection matching the preferences of the user. [3] Depending on the user model the adaptive hypermedia system will guide the learner what to read and learn and will change the content of the pages accordingly. The methods and techniques used for this are adaptive navigation support and adaptive presentation.

## Adaptive Navigation Support

In order to present the content to the learner the link-level adaptation adapts the structure of the navigation path to the user model of every learner. The navigation support changes the link structure, the link destination and how these links are presented.

In [4] we find a classification of the Adaptive Navigation Support (see Figure 2).

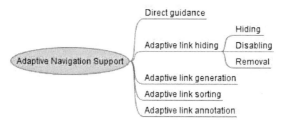

*Figure 2 Adaptive Navigation Support*

With direct guidance the student is lead to the following step by a "next" or "continue" button. In the case of showing many links the method may be adaptive link hiding, which disables or removes irrelevant links. Link anchors can be represented in different ways (wording, style and appearance) depending on their importance by link annotation. If a list of links is presented, these can be sorted by their importance.

## Adaptive content presentation

Adaptive navigation adapts the content following the goals, knowledge background, knowledge level, learning styles and another information from the learner model. For example a beginner may require some explanation for a technical term or need a simple version of a course, while another one might prefer a more a complex version. Depending on their preferences some learners might prefer text, while others learn easier with audio material or any other media format.

Figure 3 shows Peter Brusilovsky's adaptive presentation taxonomy and the 3 categories of adaptive presentation. Adaptive multimedia presentation is the manipulation of multimedia content like video or image quality and size. Adaptation of modality is the selection of the type of media and the most used text presentation. Natural language adaptation is still hard to implement; so-called canned text adaptation relies on methods like inserting and removing fragments of (conditional) text, altering fragments, stretch text, sorting fragments and dimming fragments.

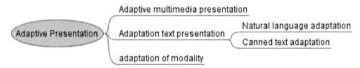

*Figure 3 Adaptive Content Presentation*

## Adaptive e-learning systems

Adaptive hypermedia systems are used in domains like e-learning, e-commerce, e-government. The most popular adaptive hypermedia systems are web–based systems. In the new dimension of the internet age, e-learning is used interchangeably in a wide variety of contexts, from companies to secondary schools and universities.

In contrast to traditional e-learning and face to face education systems which deliver the content of the course in the same way for every student adaptive educational hypermedia systems adapt to the learner. The course is adapted after the learner's goals, abilities, needs, interests, and knowledge, as defined by the user model. The adaptive system provides hyperlinks that are most relevant to the user.

Some of the adaptive hypermedia systems used in e-learning are AHA!, Interbook, KnowledgeSea.

# STATE OF THE ART E-LEARNING SYSTEMS

The variety of e-learning system can be divided under many paradigms. A recent study [22] divides the systems into popular and adaptive systems. The following paragraphs highlight a few of the systems investigated.

## E-learning Systems

Moodle is a free e-learning software platform also known as a learning management system (LMS). It supports trainers and teachers to create online courses Since it is open source software people may develop additional functionality.

Dokeos is course management system (CMS) and evolved from the LMS "Claroline". Dokeos is based on an open source business model with open code, community development and professional consulting.

Sakai is an educational platform software. It is used for teaching, research, and collaboration; it is a CMS and LMS.

Interbook is a tool for authoring and delivering adaptive electronic textbooks on the World Wide Web. Interbook applies principles of adaptive hypertext and hypermedia. It has an individual learner model for every user and provides adaptive navigation support and adaptive help.

ELM-ART is an updated version of the ELM-PE system. ELM-ART is an adaptive hypermedia system and has data about the learner in the user model, called student model and provides adaptive techniques. The last version of ELM-ART has been combined with NetCoach, an authoring tool for developing web based courses. NetCoach enables authors to create adaptive web courses based on a multi-layered model [8].

## Comparison

Most adaptive systems are used in research to test and implement new adaptive techniques, but they lack the rich interface for the user (student).

Adaptive e-learning systems provide adaptive guiding, link annotation, link hiding and adaptive presentation support. But they provide fewer features for collaboration (chat, audio and video conferencing). They do not invite human interaction or strengthen individuals' social networks. [22]

In CMS or LMS do not provide adaptive features, but they have a rich interface. They usually also provide communication tools and tools for collaborative elearning as you can see in Figure 4.

| System / Feature | dakeos | moodle | sakai | Interbook | ELM-ART | AHA |
|---|---|---|---|---|---|---|
| chat | X | X | X | | | |
| Audio conference | X | *) | *) | | | |
| Video conference | X | *) | *) | | | |
| Adaptive Guiding | | | | X | X | X |
| Link Annotation | | | | X | X | X |
| Adaptive Pres. Support | | | | X | | X |

*Table 1. Features of e-Learning Systems [22]*

AHA! is an adaptive hypermedia system that can be applied in many areas, but it was only used in the educational area for delivering adaptive courses at Eindhoven University. The first version was developed in 1998, based on the AHAM model [23].

AHA! provides adaptive presentation support, adaptive navigation support and link annotation. The adaptive presentation includes adaptive multimedia presentation, adaptive text presentation and adaptation on modality. The adaptive text presentation initially was the most unique feature of the system with, inserting and removing fragments, altering fragments, stretch text and dimming fragments.

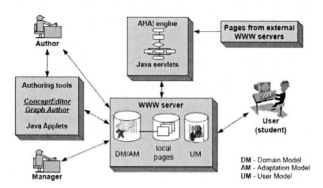

*Figure 4 AHA! Architecture[21]*

We chose to use AHA!, because it is one of the leading adaptive systems used in research and there is other research going on in the research group that includes AHA!.

## SOCIAL CONNECTEDNESS

### Definition

Social Connectedness is a psychological term used for defining the type, the quality and the number of connections we have with other people. Those connections can be in our real life or online, in our social circle, at work or in our family.

There are three general social needs: reciprocity, diversity and extensiveness. Reciprocity describes the need for reciprocal relationships in which to help and have impact on others. Diversity focuses primarily on the need for connections with people from different age groups and extensiveness is the need to be connected with a number of people [8]. There are barriers for connectedness like losing track, forgetfulness and the fears of imposing on others.

Communities have a variety of equipment in various applications for helping them communicate: telephone, mobile phone, computers, internet video-conferencing, etc., there is outpouring of energy and creativity of using information and communication technologies [9].

There is a relationship between connectedness, awareness and social presence. Social presence refers to the learner's attendance and activity in the community. Awareness is the human perception and cognitive reaction to a condition [10].

Connectedness has been described as the feeling of being "in touch" It describes a fundamental need of belonging and promotes social relationships. Connectedness is related to, but not identical with the concept of 'social presence'—the awareness that others are present. Social presence conveys the impression of connectedness, but active contact with others is necessary for true connectedness.

## Enabling social connectedness in e-learning

In an e-learning system the student is in front of the computer alone, they are not spending time with other students, or sit in a class with their peers. E-Learners are not in touch with another or aware of the social presence of the other students. The benefits of existing and learning in a community and the feature of collaboration learning are not available.

Some e-learning systems provide collaboration features. They provide for example a chat in their system or a tool for a video conference. In adaptive hypermedia systems these features are not supported. In [11] there is presented the way for enabling communication in e-learning by using asynchronous (e-mail, discussion boards and blog/weblogs) and synchronous (chat, instant messaging and audio and video web-based conferencing) communication tools.

In traditional education, students are sometimes grouped together, creating teams and working at projects. In a team the members have a common purpose, have interdependent performance goals and share an approach to work.

Virtual teams are groups of individuals who work across time, space, using communication technology. Members of virtual teams communicate electronically and they have a common purpose, have interdependent performance goals and share an approach to work.

In an adaptive hypermedia system it is possible to create virtual teams between students with the same goals, with the same preferences for a communication tool, with the same knowledge level because we have the user model with information about the student.

To bring the two aspects together- adaptive hypermedia systems and social connectedness- one can either try to introduce adaptivity to the popular but non-adaptive systems that are oriented towards social interaction, or introduce a social interaction component to the adaptive systems. This research aims at the latter.

## How we enable social connectedness in adaptive e-learning

As previously mentioned some of the e-learning systems use an internal communication tool and users have to be logged into the system to use it. But rarely all learners are going to be logged in at the same time. Trying to collaborate in e-learning is difficult, because of the students need to synchronize and being online in the system at the same time. The grouping of students is necessary. Even if some of them are logged in at the same time they might not be at the appropriate knowledge level, have different learning goals or learning styles. Creating the virtual team is difficult and is handmade most of the time. In addition to that, learners might have to get familiar with tools they have not used before.

People already use so-called Web 2.0 tools for communication in everyday life and they are often logged in at their preferred communication tool most of the day. They communicate with friends or with their classmates. We are going to use this; rather than developing tools running inside an e-learning system, we suggest making peers available for contact through their already used communication tools. The peers made available can be adapted following a set of criteria such as knowledge level, preferred communication tools or learning styles.

Tools suitable for social connectedness need to support a feeling of "being in touch" [10]. The degree of connectedness can vary between co-presence, an awareness of others, co-location, the feeling of being in the same place as others and perceived access to another intelligence, the feeling of having someone else for support within reach [15]

The tools used to support social connectedness can be divided into the different categories: chat, web conferencing tools and text messaging tools. Each tool category is represented by at least one commonly used program. The chat function is represented by the internet messenger, Skype and Yahoo! messenger. Skype is an example for a web conferencing tool. Users can leave their mobile phone number to be available for other learners to contact them.

## Web 2.0 Tools

*Web 2.0 Tools*

Web 2.0 describes a trend in the use of the World Wide Web technology and from the area of web design. In [13] O'Reilly explains that the web 2.0 term appeared in 2004 in a brainstorming in preparation for a conference. They were seeing a lot of value web applications appearing. They formulated their understanding of web 2.0 by a comparison between web 2.0 and what they called web 1.0. Table 1 shows this comparison by means of a comparison of different technologies and tools.

| Web 1.0 | | Web 2.0 |
|---|---|---|
| DoubleClick | --> | Google AdSense |
| Ofoto | --> | Flickr |
| Akamai | --> | BitTorrent |
| mp3.com | --> | Napster |
| Britannica Online | --> | Wikipedia |
| personal websites | --> | blogging |
| evite | --> | upcoming.org and EVDB |
| domain name speculation | --> | search engine optimization |
| page views | --> | cost per click |
| screen scraping | --> | web services |
| publishing | --> | participation |
| content management systems | --> | wikis |
| directories (taxonomy) | --> | tagging ("folksonomy") |
| stickiness | --> | syndication |

*Table 2. Web 1.0 vs. Web 2.0[13]*

Looking at social media [12] it seems that the evolution of online conversation models drives the increase in variety and volume as shown in figure 5. Web 1.0 was referring to personal publishing, the websites were containers for information where. There were writers and readers, but no mix of those two roles. Web 2.0 is referring to the social media, where personal conversation is the goal, using e.g. blogs or activity streams. Connectedness- where a person and their activities is present to one another and communication are the focus now. Figure 5 shows how online conversation moved on from personal publishing to online conversation and a constant change of the roles of readers and writers.

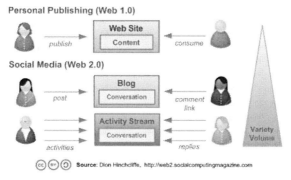

*Figure 5 Evolution Online Conversation[12]*

The impact of web 2.0 tools on education is visible. Web 2.0 is more than a set of important technologies and services or rich interface applications. Web 2.0 tools bring powerful ideas or drivers that are changing the way people interact, obtain knowledge and some of them are the indirect reflection of the power of the networks [14].

*Skype*

Skype was founded in 2003 by Niklas Zennstrom and Janus Friis. Skype is a free software for VoIP and is available in 28 languages [16, 17]. Figure 6 shows a screenshot of the skype interface.

*Figure 6 Skype interface*

Free features of skype are skype-to-skype calls, transfer calls, instant messaging and group chats, conference calls with up to nine people, forward calls to people on skype and for a buy Skype credit you can call phones and mobiles or can sent short text message. Now skype can be use and on WIFI phone[16] as well. The total number of total user accounts in Q1 2008 was 309.3 millions [17]. These features, in particular the free skype-to-skype calls, the availability on mobile phones and the high number of users makes it a suitable tool for the ***Connect!*** module.

*Twitter*

Twitter is a free social networking and micro-blogging service that allows users to send updates or send messages to one another. The sender can restrict the sending of the message and update just to some people and users can receive updates, send messages via the twitter website, send instant messages, text messages and use RSS feeds, email or other supporting applications such as Twitterrific or facebook [18]. Figure 7 shows a screenshot of the Twitter interface.

*Figure 7 Twitter interface*

In March 2008 the total number of users was 1+ million, the total active Users was 200,000 per week and the total Twitter Messages was 3 million/day [19].

*IM MSN*

Instant Messenger MSN (or Windows Live Messenger) is a freeware instant messaging client that was developed and distributed by Microsoft. Since February 2006 it is a part of Microsoft's Windows Live series of online services and software.

Features of IM MSN include the possibility to connect with Yahoo messenger, PC to PC calling, video conversation, sharing folders, send messages to mobile devices, receive Windows live alerts. In November 2007 IM MSN registered 294 million active users worldwide [20].

*Figure 8 IM MSN interface*

Figure 8 shows a screenshot of the IM MSN interface.

*IM Yahoo*

Yahoo Messenger is an instant messenger provided by Yahoo. It is provided free of charge and can be downloaded and used with a generic "Yahoo ID". IM Yahoo offers PC-to-PC, PC-to-Phone and phone-to-PC services, file transfers, webcam hosting, text messaging service, and chat rooms in various categories. Figure 9 shows a screenshot of the IM Yahoo interface.

*Figure 9 IM Yahoo interface*

# CONNECT!

## Requirements

The requirements for ***Connect!*** include a list of assessment items as input for the adaptation engine. From the user model of the adaptive hypermedia system the knowledge level of every student is needed. We need the username of three communication tools and the preferred ranking of these tools. The digital literacy is assessed by a special questionnaire. The adaptive engine then assigns groups of student after these criteria.

## Framework

As mentioned the user model information will be taken from the adaptive learning system, as well as the learning style for every student. Otherwise the *Connect!* module assesses the learning style via ILS questionnaire.

This is combined with information collected from the student in an assessment for the *Connect!* module. This information covers a list of communication tools, a ranking of these tools, both required to adapt to tools preferences of the learner. Self-perceived skills using the internet and time spent online as well as years of internet use provide information on the digital literacy.

The framework has communication adaptation rules. The adaptive engine of the module provides the contact for the selected group using the web 2.0 tools used for communication.   We have the username of every student for up to 3 preferred tools and we have and the communication tools interfaces. Figure 10 shows the framework for the *Connect!* module.

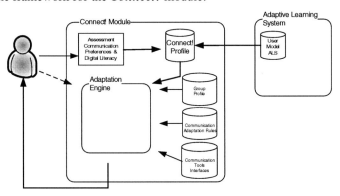

*Figure 10 Framework Connect! module*

The *Connect!* module stores all the required information in the *Connect!* profile database. The adaptation engine requests input from the *Connect!* profile database. The adaptation engine then retrieves the adaptation rules from the *Connect!* adaptation rules database, considering the information in the *Connect!* profile as outlined above and the rules about group size. The group size is set at a minimum of 2 learners and a maximum of six learners [24]. Once the adaptation selects suitable peers and the tools to connect with them, suitable tools interfaces are taken from **Connect!** tool database. The combination of tools interfaces and adaptation rules generates the response to the user who is provided with a list of suitable peers and an interface to directly contact them in the selected tool. This group information is stored in a group profile which is updated after each assessment, or after the time that the tutor said the is needed to achieve the knowledge of a concept [3].

# SYSTEM IMPLEMENTATION

## Technical landscape of technologies used

The **Connect!** module is a web-based adaptive engine, build on Java Servlet technology and works with the Apache /Tomcat server. **Connect!** was tested and integrated with AHA!, a well-researched adaptive platform.

It has a 3-layer architecture. The user interface layer contains the information how the communication tool will appear to the student, the business layer contains information on the adaptation engine and the logical layer contains the information for the ConnectServlet. In the DB layer, all the data is stored in an XML file.

The user interface layer integrates 3 servlets; a LoginServlet that creates the session and puts all the data for the **Connect!** module into the session, the data that is needed for the session in AHA! and the data needed by the RedirectServlet. The Login Servlet will redirect to the RedirectServlet.

The **Connect!** module needs a Student Object. The Student Object contains all the data that is needed by the ConnectServlet, e.g. name of the student, and the id of the group where the adaptive engine put the learner.

The AHA! system needs the login username for the session, the name of the course, the directory and the active concept for the learner.

The ConnectServlet take from the session the data needed, e.g. the student login or student id and the group ID and receives the content for the web server, the HTML and javascript content for embedding the tool of the student group from the Logical Layer for **Connect!**.

The RedirectServlet will retrieve the RedirectContent from the web server. The RedirectContent is the HTML that will have two iframes and one iframe will redirect to ConnectServlet and another one redirects to AHA!.

## Adaptive Engine Architecture

We know the knowledge level for every student, the 3 preferred tools used by that student, the learning style and the level of computer literacy. The goal is to put the student in the right group, that is the group of students with the same knowledge level, the same tool preference, learning style and level of computer literacy.

Initially the aim is to put the student in the right group, but if there are no other student with a matching set of criteria, the selection process goes back step by step.

At first the students are matched according to their knowledge level. ***Connect!*** has the possibility to put student in 6 different knowledge level groups (see figure 11).

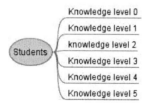

*Figure 11 Knowledge Level Groups*

After the students are divided into groups according to their knowledge level they are divided into another 4 groups according to their preferred communication tool. Figure 12 shows this for the learners form the group with knowledge level 0.

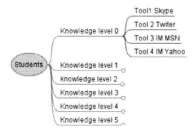

*Figure 12 Knowledge Level - Tool Groups*

Students from each group are then divided in groups according to the learning style as shown in figure 13.

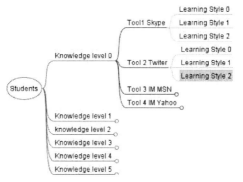

*Figure 13 Knowledge Level - Tool - Learning Styles Groups*

And finally the students are assigned to their group according to computer literacy level (see figure 14).

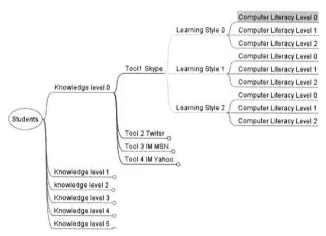

*Figure 14 Knowledge Level - Tool - Learning Styles - Computer Literacy Group*

Now every student is in the right group. The next step is to see if the number of students in a computer literacy group is 1, between 2 and 6, or more than 6. Groups of 2 to 6 are the target and the system aims to keep groups stable.

If there is just one student the system can't create a group, therefore the student is maintained in a flag. If there is more than one student the system checks to see if there is another student in the flag and if their criteria match, except for the last level considered. If there are between two and six students the system creates a group. The group information contains the knowledge level, the tool, the learning style, the computer literacy of the group and a list of the student IDs of the students in the group.

If there is just one person in a tool group the system tries to find a place in the same knowledge level group and if that does not work the system checks whether there is a group available on a knowledge level group +-1 the originally selected level.

If there is no group for a student, and there is just one person in the knowledge level group the system puts that student in contact with a teacher.

The whole process is depicted in the flowchart in figure 15.

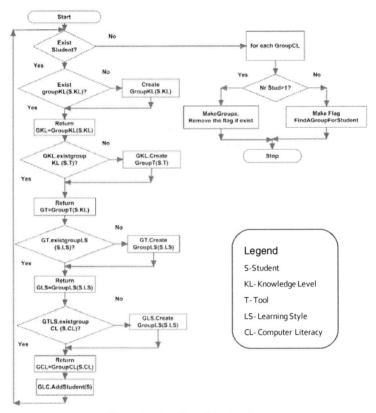

*Figure 15 Flowchart Selection Process*

## Case Study

The ***Connect!*** module was integrated into the AHA! system. The course used is the AHA! tutorial. ***Connect!*** was tested with a small group of learners, some of the summer school students and some post docs in the lab.

After logging in the user ioanas, a student at knowledge level 2 and her preferred tool is skype, her learning style is known and her computer literacy Level is 1. All the rest of the students have the same knowledge level, tool preferences, computer literacy, and learning style. Figure 16 shows the tutorial after login. The frame on the left is the ***Connect!*** module, the tutorial is in the big frame on the right

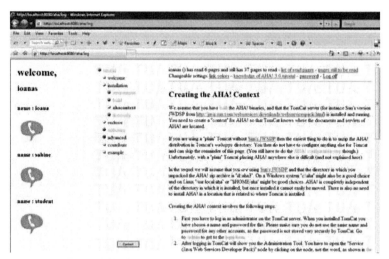

*Figure 16 Welcome page AHA! and Connect! user ioanas*

If the user ioanas clicks on one of the skype icons the skype application is invoked and a link is created between the 2 learners. They could talk, have a video conference, a board meeting or a chat.

*Figure 17 User Ioanas Connect! to other users*

Gioana is a student at knowledge level 4, learning style 3, computer literacy 0, and the preferred tool is twitter. She decides to contact another student with a text message.

When she clicks on the twitter tool a window with the twitter interface appears in the browser and she is able to send text messages (see figure 18).

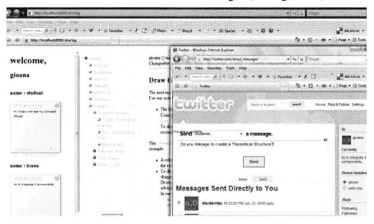

*Figure 18 AHA+ **Connect!**+ twitter, user: gioana*

## CONCLUSION AND FUTURE WORK

This research combines for the first time considerations of social connectedness, and adaptivity in adaptive e-learning systems. The proposed *Connect!* module enables continuous social interaction, supporting users of adaptive e-learning systems. The students awareness about the presence of other students in the same learning place can be increased.

One of the benefits is that the learners use tools that they are already familiar with and this improves the accessibility among the learners. Another benefit is that the students can communicate even if some of them are not logged in the system.

We intend to test the *Connect!* with secondary school students and with students in a third level institution to compare the learning results of the students.

I intend to continue with the research on AHA! and *Connect!* at my diploma project this year

The *Connect!* module is part of a research project investigating how to improve the quality of experience (QoE) of learners in adaptive multimedia systems. The improved communication options will make a contribution towards QoE. This project has been implemented in a research internship during the Online Dublin Computer Science Summer School (ODCSSS) at DCU.

## REFERENCES

[1] Paul De Bra, Ad Aerts, David Smits, Natalia Stash(2002), "AHA! The next generation " in *Proceedings of the thirteenth ACM conference on Hypertext and hypermedia*, College Park, Maryland, USA.

[2] Peter Brusilovsky(2000), Adaptive Hypermedia: "From Intelligent Tutoring Systems to Web-Based Education" in *Intelligent Tutoring Systems,* Last retrieved 20 August 2008 from http://www.springerlink.com/content/dnt2272vmw6wjfar/fulltext.pdf .

[3]Sabine Moebs, Jenifer McManis(2008), " Adaptive Social Connectedness in a multimedia e-learning environment "in *China-Ireland Conference on Information and Communications Technologies 2008.*

[4] Brusilowsky, P. (2001), "Adaptive Hypermedia" in *User Modeling and User-Adapted interaction* 11:87-110,Netherlands, Klenwer Academic Publishers, p. 100.

[5] Torstein Rekkedal & Svein Qvist-Eriksen (2003), "Internet Based E-learning, Pedagogy and Support Systems" Last retrieved 20 August 2008 from http://www.fernuni-hagen.de/ZIFF/ZP_121.pdf#page=14.

[6] Clark, R. C. & Mayer R. (2003), "e-Learning and the Science of Instruction: Proven Guidelines for Consumers and Designers of Multimedia Learning", San Francisco, CA: Pfeiffer.

[7] Sabine Moebs, "A good Mix in blended Learning For Small and Medium sized Enterprises, in particular from the IT and Tourism Industry", Last retrieved 20 August 2008 from http://www.specialtrees.net/BL4SMEs_MSc/SMoebs_MSc_ExecSummary.pdf.

[8] Margaret Morris, Jay Lundell, Eric Dishman,(2004)"Catalyzing Social Interaction with Ubiquitous Computing: A needs assessment of elders coping with cognitive decline",  in *CHI '04 extended abstracts on human factors in computing system*, pages 1151 – 1154.

[9] Linda Phipps(2000), "A conduit for social inclusion, New Communications Technologies", in *Information Communication & Society*, Volume 3, Issue 1, pages 39 – 68.

[10] R. Rettie ,(2003) "Connectedness Awareness and Social Presence" in *Proceedings 6th International Workshop on Presence*, Retrieved 5 June 2008 from http://www.presence-research.org/p2003.html.

[11] Repman, J., Carlson, R. & Zinskie, C. (2004), "Interactive Communication Tools in E-Learning: What Works?" In *Proceedings of World Conference on E-Learning in Corporate, Government, Healthcare, and Higher Education 2004* (pp. 1443-1448). Chesapeake, VA: AACE.

[12] Dion Hinchcliffe,(2008)," Endless Conversation: The Unfolding Saga of Blogs, Twitter, Friendfeed, and Social Sites" from http://web2.wsj2.com/ .

[13] Tim O'Reilly (2005), What Is Web 2.0 - Design Patterns and Business Models for the Next Generation of Software from http://www.oreillynet.com/pub/a/oreilly/tim/news/2005/09/30/what-is-web-20.html .

[14] Paul Andreson (2007), "What is web 2.0? Ideas, technologies and implication for education", in *JISC Technology and Standards Watch*.

[15] F. Biocca, J. Burgoon, C. Harms, M. Stoner (2003). "Criteria and scope conditions for a theory and measure of social presence", in *Presence: Teleoperators & Virtual Environments*, Vol. 12, No. 5, pp. 456–480.

[16] http://www.skype.com/intl/en/features/.

[17] Jim Courtney (2008) Skype's Q! Results Demonstate Voice, But Business Grows from http://www.entrepreneur.com/technology/managingtechnology/web20columnistfrankbell/article181082.html .

[18] Frank Bell (2007), Web 2.0 Tools for Getting Noticed 2007 from http://www.entrepreneur.com/technology/managingtechnology/web20columnistfrankbell/article181082.html.

[19] Michael Arrington (2008), End of Speculation: the real twitter usage numbers, from http://www.techcrunch.com/2008/04/29/end-of-speculation-the-real-twitter-usage-numbers/ .

[20] http://en.wikipedia.org/wiki/Instant_messaging.

[21] Paul De Bra, Ad Aerts, Bart Berden, Barend de Lange, Brendan Rousseau, Tomi Santic, David Smits, Natalia Stash(2003), AHA! The Adaptive Hypermedia Architecture, Last retrieved 20 August 2008 http://wwwis.win.tue.nl/~debra/ht03/pp401-debra.pdf

[22] D. Hauger, M. Kock(2007) "State of the Art of Adaptivity in E-Learning Platforms", *in  Proceedings 15th Workshop on Adaptivity and User Modeling in Interactive Systems* (ABIS), pp. 355-360.

[23] Hongjing Wu, Geert-Jan Houben, Paul DeBra (1998), "AHAM: A Reference Model to Support Adaptive Hypermedia Authoring " Last retrieved on 20 August 2008 http://wwwis.win.tue.nl/~debra/infwet98/paper.pdf

[24] David W. Johnson & Roger T. Johnson & Karl Smith,"The State of Cooperative Learning in Postsecondaryand Professional Settings"

# INCREASING EFFICIENCY OF HYBRID BUSINESS PROCESSES IN THE MANUFACTURING INDUSTRY USING A PROCESS DECENTRALIZING APPROACH

Dinh Khoa Nguyen, Master Student at the Institute of Computer Science, University of Heidelberg, Heidelberg, Germany, dinhkhoanguyen@gmail.com, Tel: +49 176 24210342

Patrik Spieß, SAP Research, Vincenz-Prießnitz-Strasse 1, D-76131, Karlsruhe, Germany, patrik.spiess@sap.com, Tel +49 6227 770617

Jürgen Rückert, Software Engineering Group, Institute of Computer Science, University of Heidelberg, D-69120 Heidelberg, Germany, rueckert@informatik.uni-heidelberg.de, Tel +49 6221 545815

Barbara Paech, Software Engineering Group, Institute of Computer Science, University of Heidelberg, D-69120 Heidelberg, Germany, paech@informatik.uni-heidelberg.de, Tel +49 6221 545810

## ABSTRACT

*There is a recent trend in the manufacturing industry that shop-floor[1] ubiquitous devices (such as smart embedded devices, RFIDs, sensors, etc.) are becoming more powerful regarding computing and communication resources, up to the point where they can directly offer their functionalities as web services. This capability of ubiquitous devices brings them closer to novel hybrid business processes, which can be modelled as an orchestration of several service interactions with hybrid systems using the Business Process Description Language (BPEL). However, conventional centralized BPEL execution is known as a heavy and inefficient approach, especially in the manufacturing industry, where each cross-layer service interaction can go through several heterogeneous and unreliable network layers. This paper explores the feasibility and advantages of a decentralizing approach which partitions and distributes a BPEL process to the shop-floor level, to increase the locality and reliability of the BPEL executions. Reference implementations for the runtime platforms for this approach are also suggested in this paper.*

---

[1] In manufacturing, the shop-floor is where machines are located and products are produced

*Keywords: SOA for Manufacturing, Hybrid Business Process, Distributed BPEL Orchestration, Reliability on the Shop-Floor, Embedded Systems.*

## INTRODUCTION

The Service Oriented Architecture (SOA) paradigm is recently the modern trend of software development, where enterprise's survival requires constant changes through innovations to adapt to market demands. Using web services as a single communication standard between software components, a SOA system could ensure not only the flexibility with respect to. rapid change of technologies, but also the interoperability of cross-system and cross-organization integrations. Following the SOA concept, business experts claimed that organizing a business process by modelling it as an orchestration of web service interactions allows tight integration of process steps and more flexibility in changing the process later. Such a workflow is executed by a process engine which orchestrates coarse-grained web services offered by enterprise applications such as Customer Relationship Management, Supply Chain Management, Enterprise Resource Planning, etc. The workflows are modelled in an executable process language so that they can be executed by a process engine. At the moment, BPEL (Web Service Business Process Execution Language 2.0, 2007) is the dominant language for formulating executable descriptions of business processes.

The next leap in the evolution of business processes in the manufacturing industry is foreseen as the integration of ubiquitous technology into business processes. Currently, networked embedded systems are widely used. Standard, IP-based communication is replacing proprietary or domain-specific communication, especially within manufacturing at shop-floor level. Some technologies such as manufacturing automation, industrial robots, RFID, etc., have been developed and applied intensively in the industry. Others like wireless sensor (and actor) networks, ubiquitous computing technology are on the brink of leaving research labs and being used productively. Those shop-floor devices are becoming more powerful regarding computing and communication resources, and hence could be used as autonomous smart items which completely encapsulate some tasks. As we are moving towards an Internet of Things (Fleisch, E. and Mattern F., 2005), we would also like to integrate those shop-floor devices into enterprise business processes, to enable more flexibility and adaptability in shop-floor level by including some business intelligence already at a technical level as low as that.

Given a complete service-oriented manufacturing landscape, such a cross-layer hybrid business process can be modelled using the BPEL modelling language and executed by a BPEL execution engine. However, conventional BPEL processes are known as a heavily centralized orchestration of multiple cross-layer WS, which causes some inefficiencies for manufacturing. In section 2, this paper addresses exactly these inefficiencies and suggests applying the distributed BPEL orchestration approach to tackle them. In section 3, some open source runtime platforms are suggested to be used for the implementation of this approach. Section 4 summarizes the paper and introduces further research issues that we intend to tackle in future.

# DECENTRALIZATION OF HYBRID BUSINESS PROCESSES USING DISTRIBUTED BPEL ORCHESTRATION

In this section, we focus on a top-down approach of process decentralization, namely the partitioning of a centralized hybrid BPEL process into smaller fragments and distributing them to the shop-floor. Our goal is to support business designers to model their initial BPEL processes freely, without knowing much about the underlying sophisticated cross-layer network topology, and then improve the process efficiency using this partitioning and distribution approach.

We first explain in the first subsection why the conventional centralized BPEL orchestration is inefficient for the manufacturing regarding the performance (response time and system throughput), reliability and scalability. The next subsection describes the distributed BPEL orchestration as an approach to tackle the inefficiencies, as well as some related issues of applying this approach.

## Problems of centralized BPEL processes in cross-layer manufacturing landscape

The SOA paradigm has brought the shop-floor devices closer to the enterprise computing by turning them into SOA-ready devices and integrating them directly into hybrid executable business processes described e.g. in BPEL. BPEL provides simple coordination among shop-floor services and transparent access to them. However, BPEL is restricted to a heavily centralized approach because the process is executed only by a single coordinator engine. It receives input data from client, coordinates the data flow and control flow among cross-layer services to produce output data for the client, and invoke each service as specified in the process description. The following Figure 1 depicts a simple centralized BPEL production process flowing through the shop-floors of a manufacturing plant, packaging plant and logistics provider.

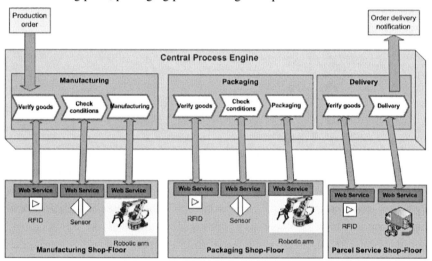

*Figure 1: Centralized Hybrid BPEL Process*

The process coordinator, a BPEL process engine, hosts a BPEL hybrid production process as described in the figure. It receives from the client a production order for the package of material goods that has already arrived at the manufacturing plant. In the production request there is also other information, like the order id, which can be read from a RFID chip, and the condition thresholds, e.g. temperature and shock level, which can be read from a sensor attached to the package. RFID, sensor and the robotic arm are SOA-enabled shop-floor devices, so that they can be directly invoked by the BPEL engine over WS communication during a process execution. After the whole process flows through all three service partners successfully, an order delivery confirmation will be notified to the client.

In general, a centralized BPEL execution must face several problems regarding performance, reliability and scalability, which are explained in the following issues:

- **(I1)** First, there is too much network communication between the coordinator BPEL engine and the service components, which might increase the network congestion and transfer latency. It is even worse when the system lacks a fast and stable network connection like Ethernet, e.g. a mobile environment with a high number of connected nodes, and several problems such as roaming, frequent disconnections and security (Maurino et al. 2005).

- **(I2)** Chafle et al. (2004) claimed that the coordinator engine in the centralized approach might become a performance bottleneck because it must serve every service invocation of a process instance. Considering the whole system is under high load, which means that a lot of instances are being coordinated by the engine, the situation might get worse and the coordinator engine becomes overloaded. As a result, the system throughput would be reduced and the execution time of each instance would increase.

- **(I3)** Considering the data flow within a BPEL process, Chafle et al. (2004) also presented the inefficiency of sending back response data to the coordinator engine after a service invocation is successfully processed at a service node. Rather, data should be able to be sent directly from the provider node to the consumer node[2] through peer-to-peer communication. It saves time and network traffic, and reduces the work load on the coordinator engine as well.

- **(I4)** In the Business-To-Business circumstance, each business contributes to the global success of the process, but also has the discipline to hide the internal business operations. A centralized approach would, in contrast, have to know the details how to execute each process step.

---

[2] Provider node is a service node that processes a service invocation of a process step to produce output data for the next steps. Consumer node is in contrast, the service node which processes a process step using data produced by the previous process steps

A hybrid business process in the manufacturing domain might be executed in a cross-layer landscape, in which the gap between shop-floor devices and the central process engine may contain many sophisticated and heterogeneous network layers. Interaction messages must be routed through unstable, frequently disrupted layers like Wi-Fi or tunnelled through secure but expensive and long-delay ones like VPN. Although the communication standard is over SOAP, each network layer requires a specific underlying protocol for routing and tunnelling, which introduces more overhead and delay. In each step of the process, a cross-layer service interaction is executed by sending and receiving SOAP messages through these layers, as depicted in the following Figure 2.

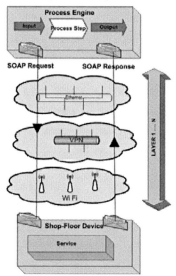

*Figure 2: Cross-layer service invocation*

This characteristic increases the inefficiencies (I1) & (I3) of the centralized BPEL execution, because the service interactions between the central engine and the shop-floor services could become slower, e.g. due to the high-latency routing layers, or more unreliable, e.g. due to low-quality Wi-Fi. One can easily recognize that too much network traffic, in case the process has large-scale sequential interaction steps, would also cause more network congestion and consequently, the service interactions would also be strongly affected.

## Distributed BPEL Orchestration To The Shop-Floor

Understanding the inefficiencies of the centralized BPEL process execution, distributed BPEL orchestration is an approach that could solve the mentioned issues. The approach partitions the initial process into process fragments and then distributes them to multiple locations. Each process fragment is executed by a local process engine, which means the central engine is now only responsible for coordinating the local engines and not the whole process. The following Figure 3 explains how the production process in Figure 1 can be distributed to several locations

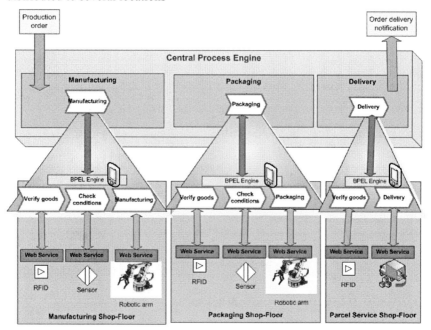

*Figure 3: Distributing BPEL Orchestration To The Shop-Floor*

We assume that in the shop-floors of a manufacturing plant, packaging plant and the parcel service, there are PDAs equipped with local BPEL engines. These PDAs are kept by a Shop-Floor Manager at each plant who is responsible for the local execution at that place. The original production process can then be partitioned into three fragments: manufacturing, packaging and delivery. Each fragment is now executed locally at each plant's shop-floor by the local BPEL engine hosted on the PDA, and the results are sent back after the local execution completes. In order to coordinate the distributed fragments of a process instance, correlation data is used. The correlation data must be distributed to process fragments as well, and after a fragment finishes its execution, the correlation data must be included in the output sent back to the central engine, in order to indicate, to which process instance this distributed execution belongs.

For instance, the PDA at the manufacturing shop-floor hosts a local BPEL process that orchestrates a distributed process fragment containing the verification, conditions checking and manufacturing steps. It receives from the main process instance the order id as the correlation data. Lastly, after the execution completes, it informs the central engine that the manufacturing of this order id is finished. The central engine receives the notification, checks the correlation data (the order id) and delegates the notification to the right process instance to trigger the packaging fragment at the packaging shop-floor.

In a more realistic scenario, industrial single board computers (SBC), which are located near the shop-floor devices in each manufacturing section, can be used to host BPEL engines to execute local BPEL executions. The Shop-Floor manager uses his PDA only for coordinating and managing the SBCs in the whole manufacturing plant.

In the following, we first point out the motivating advantages of this BPEL partitioning and distribution approach. Then we consider the essential data flow analysis before the partitioning and the partitioning rules for exception handling in BPEL. Lastly, we introduce some recent attempts for automatic BPEL transformation for this approach.

*Advantages of the BPEL partitioning and distribution approach*

First of all, the distributed BPEL orchestration directly tackles the (I1) issue in the previous subsection. By means of decentralizing the process fragments to distributed BPEL engines located in the shop-floor, it increases the locality of a process execution for better reliability, and also saves the communication between the central coordinator with shop-floor services. In Figure 3, the central coordinator has only one interaction with each service partner, instead of three in Figure 1. Saving network communication would reduce the execution time of the process, especially in case of cross-layered heterogeneous network connections.

Addressing the issue (I2), this approach reduces the loads at the central coordinator by distributing the loads to multiple local engines. However, it seems to be reasonable only for the powerful local engines to host and execute large and complex fragments. In case a BPEL engine is only available on a resource constrained node, its constrained capacity may cause bottleneck again, which reduces the throughput and increases execution time.

In principle, this approach does not solve the issue (I3) because each web service still has to send the response back to the coordinator node. The improvement here is only that the responses are only sent back to local coordinators, which is clearly more efficient than sending back to the central one. Moreover, a local BPEL engine must also send back the outputs of the process fragments to the central engine, while in the other more ideal solutions, the outputs might be transferred directly to the next local BPEL engine.

The issue (I4) is perfectly solved with this distribution approach. Using a local BPEL engine as a proxy service to the outside, each business partner can contribute his business outcomes to a B2B process, without letting the outside world know how these values were created. For instance in Figure 3, the manufacturing shop-floor might be able to hide its internal manufacturing process behind its BPEL engine. From the outside, one can talk only with the Shop-Floor Manager with his PDA.

*Data flow analysis*

However, the BPEL distribution approach only retains the original control dependencies among the process steps. Concerning the data flow, the original centralized process should only be partitioned when a clean analysis of data dependencies among the process steps has been done before. In BPEL, data are stored in variables and variables belong to scopes. A process step in a scope can only get access to the variables of that scope or the enclosing scopes. To distribute a process fragment within a scope to another location, one must analyze which variables in which scopes are relevant to that fragment and then distribute them too. After the local execution finishes, the new variables' values are returned to the central engine and must be synchronized with other concurrent distributed BPEL executions, based on the data dependencies defined in the original process.

The data flow analysis is also quite important for the decision whether to apply BPEL distribution approach. In the following Figure 4 we analyze the worst and best case of applying BPEL distribution approach for a process fragment based on the input output data.

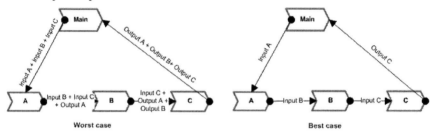

*Figure 4: Data Flow Analysis for BPEL Distribution*

In Figure 4, a process fragment containing step A, B and C is partitioned and distributed to a local engine. The steps A, B, C have Input A, B, C and Output A, B, C respectively. The worst case is depicted on the left side of the figure, when the Input A, B and C are completely different and can only be provided from the Main step, and all different Output A, B and C must be returned to the Main step. In this worst case, although there is only one service invocation from the central engine to the local engine, the exchanged data between them are really huge. Exchanging such huge data makes this invocation comparable with three sequential invocations of the initial centralized execution, regarding the network traffic and response time. Moreover, transferring large message over unstable network might be more unreliable, i.e. message could get lost or loose integrity more easily.

The most ideal case is when the distributed fragment is a completely independent sub-process within the original process. The right side of Figure 4 shows such a sub-process which receives Input A and transforms them to Output C. Such a sub-process is ideal for distribution because the process steps within it only need the input data produced by the previous steps, e.g. Input B is provided by either Input A or Output A.

*Exception handling*

We have described so far the partitioning and distribution approach for centralized BPEL processes. However, only the normal behaviours of the process have been concerned. For the unexpected behaviours occurring at runtime, BPEL supports a set of exception[3] handling mechanisms including event handler, fault handler, and compensation handler. Still missing are the partitioning rules for exception handlers, e.g. event and error delegation, error recovery, etc., and the infrastructure to implement these rules.

In BPEL, exceptions and exception handlers belong to a scope. The introduced decentralizing approach for a scope partitions it into several process fragments and distributes these fragments to several local orchestrators. The partitioning must be aware of the exception handling as well, meaning that each fragment must have new exception handling codes. When an exception within the scope is raised, it must be delegated to all involved local orchestrators. Because each local orchestrator has its own exception handling, the scope must synchronize the handling results returned from all involved orchestrators. Baresi et al. (2006) suggested using a synchronization mechanism at the end of each scope and the following exception propagation mechanism.

---

[3] We imply „Exception" to be an event or a fault and "exception handler" to be an event, fault or compensation handler

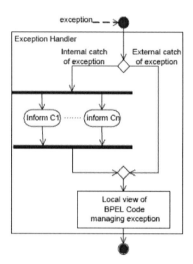

*Figure 5: Distributed Exception Handling*

Figure 5, adopted from Baresi et al. (2006), depicts the exception propagation mechanism within a BPEL scope. When an exception is raised, each distributed exception handler will receive that exception. It checks then whether the exception comes from the local execution or from other external ones. Only in the latter case, it informs other distributed orchestrators about this exception. Then, the local handling of this exception is in turn for handling the exception. As mentioned above, after all distributed handlers finish handling activities, the scope must synchronize the handling results properly by a synchronization mechanism.

*State-of-the-art in automatic BPEL transformation*

The advantages of BPEL distribution approach motivate many researchers to identify the partitioning rules for a centralized BPEL process and then automatically transform it into distributed partitions. Maurino et al. (2005) proposed an approach to describe BPEL processes in UML using an extended UML profile for automated business processes (Mantell, 2005). Using a UML model for BPEL, the authors introduced several graph transformation rules for BPEL activities such as sequence, while, flow, pick, etc. After the original centralized process is partitioned using graph transformation, the new UML models can be exported to BPEL processes, which are actually the new partitioned process fragments to be distributed. This work was improved by Baresi et al. (2006), suggesting an explicit meta model for BPEL activities to improve partitioning rules with data dependency among partitioned process fragments. The authors are also working on a tool that implements their partitioning rules and automates the whole "slicing" process. They are also working on the environment to execute such distributed BPEL processes.

Assuming that there has been enough work in automatic BPEL transformation, we decided to put our focus rather on the runtime platforms for the distributed BPEL orchestration approach. In the next section, a reference implementation for the distributed running platforms is introduced using open source SOA standards and tools.

## REFERENCE IMPLEMENTATION WITH OPEN SOURCE PLATFORMS

### Web Services on Shop-Floor Devices

Bringing Web Services on devices, flexibility to the shop floor has been heavily exploited by several well-known organizations and projects. Microsoft and a few printer companies extended this idea to embedded devices and proposed standards like Device Profile for Web Services (DPWS) (Schlimmer et al., 2006). Several European projects like the EU Project SiRENA (2005), EU Project SODA (2003) and EU Project SOCRADES (2008) joined the band wagon and extended the specifications to a low footprint embedded stack that can be directly ported on devices with limited computing resources. As a result, devices can host web services (SOA-ready devices) and proactively participate in the SOA landscape.

In the SOCRADES project, devices in the shop-floor are hosted with the DPWS stack that supports a variety of Web Service Standards. Figure 6 illustrates the WS-* protocol stacks implemented in DPWS.

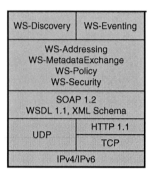

Devices Profile for Web Services
(DPWS)
protocol stack

*Figure 6: Device Profile for Web Services (DPWS) (Schlimmer et al. 2006)*

The support of WS-Discovery (2005) and WS-Eventing (2006) in DPWS introduces an advantage for shop-floor services. A DPWS service in the shop-floor can now proactively discover other DPWS service partners and collaborate with them in a peer-to-peer way via direct WS communication. It can also proactively collaborate to business processes in the application layer by notifying WS events to the process engine. Other legacy devices in the shop-floor that can be connected only through their gateway can also expose their functionalities through a DPWS-enabled gateway.

In one of the disseminations, a small footprint C language based DPWS stack can be deployed on programmable logic controllers which host generic services like starting and stopping a mechanic device like a robotic arm. Another practical implementation of DPWS web services on sensor nodes could be realized by SunSPOTs, which run a small footprint of the java virtual machine Sqwak (Sun™ Small Programmable Object Technology, 2007).

## BPEL Engine on Shop-Floor Devices

The near future of ubiquitous and pervasive computing foresees the computation and communication potential of embedded resource-constrained computing devices for deploying and executing collaborative applications. E.g., today you have a wide variety of Java-capable devices such as PDAs, mobile phones, SunSPOTs... Although there are still a lot of constraints regarding their computing and communication resources, the incorporation of these devices could explore many advantages. A motivating scenario in manufacturing automation has been already introduced in the previous Figure 3, where distributed BPEL sub-processes are desired to be hosted on Java-capable PDAs, which should be tailored with light-weight BPEL engines.

Motivated from the advantages of having a process engine on resource constrained devices, Hackmann et al. (2006 and 2007) introduced Sliver, a light-weight BPEL workflow process execution engine implemented in Java. Sliver is designed as a light-weight BPEL engine to host and execute BPEL processes on resource constrained devices. It addresses exactly the following practical issues that prevent existing BPEL middleware being deployed on devices.

- Footprint: The combined footprint of BPEL middleware with their support layers is really big for devices. Hackmann et al. (2006) claimed that Apache Tomcat 5.5.17 (including the requisite J2SE 1.4.2 runtime) consumes 78 MB of disk space and 20 MB of RAM even before a single application has been deployed. Installing the ActiveBPEL engine increases this footprint to 92 MB of disk space and 22 MB of RAM. Deploying BPEL processes on ActiveBPEL will consume even more resources. These resource consumptions are quite reasonable on back-end systems, but in contrast extremely critical for less powerful shop-floor devices.

- Runtime platform: On one hand, most of resource constrained Java-capable devices such as mobile phones support only a limited Java runtime platform, e.g. the J2ME CLDC with MIDP profile, which has very limited APIs for Java implementations. More capable runtime platforms (WebSphere Everyplace Micro Environment[4]) support J2ME CDC with Personal Profile, a runtime environment which implements almost all features of J2SE specifications. However, some of important J2SE features are still missing, especially in the network I/O APIs. On the other hand, existing BPEL engines implemented in Java most probably require a fully J2SE compatible runtime environment, especially the advanced network I/O APIs. Hence they could not operate on limited platforms or on limited devices.

---

[4] One might know it under the alias J9

- Communication Protocols: Devices may have to communicate over some proprietary protocol while BPEL engines exchange SOAP/HTTP messages over TCP/IP sockets. Hence, this problem prevents devices serving SOAP/HTTP requests.

Sliver solves these issues with its minimum footprint, its support for both J2ME and J2SE and its generic communication interfaces which can be arbitrarily implemented with any low-level proprietary protocols. Moreover, Sliver is released as an open source engine with a few third-party libraries such as kSOAP2 for parsing and constructing SOAP documents and Jetty Web Server for supporting HTTP server. Another advantage is that these libraries are actually designed for resource constrained device, too. The Sliver implementation is fully available and its design structure is quite easy to understand as well as to further develop. However, it must be emphasized that Sliver is not intended to fully replace the existing feature-full BPEL engines, because its implementation only supports the fundamental parts of the BPEL standards. Rather, it is designed for resource constrained devices which are not supported with BPEL so far.

We decided to use Sliver for the distributed BPEL orchestration because of its support for shop-floor devices and high extensibility. For a simulation prototype, we deployed Sliver on a PDA which runs the IBM WEME platform with J2ME CDC. For Web Services on devices, the deployment of DPWS on both PDA and SunSPOT was also successful. A prototype BPEL process, which interacts with DPWS services, was successfully deployed and executed in Sliver.

## SUMMARY AND FUTURE WORK

This paper discusses an optimization approach for hybrid business processes in manufacturing domain by partitioning a BPEL process into independent sub-processes and distributing them down to the shop-floor level. We explained the reasons why the conventional centralized BPEL execution is not suitable for the hybrid business processes in a cross-layer manufacturing landscape. We explored the advantages of using the distributed BPEL orchestration approach to tackle the inefficiencies of the centralized execution. Some issues regarding this approach such as data flow analysis, partitioning rules, distributed exception handling and automatic BPEL transformation were also mentioned. Lastly, we suggested deploying a DPWS stack on shop-floor devices to turn them to SOA-ready devices and deploying Sliver, an open source light-weight BPEL engine, on shop-floor devices to host and execute the distributed BPEL sub-processes.

The approach introduced in this paper could save a lot of cross-layered communication and hence, obviously improves the locality and reliability of the BPEL execution. However, some questions concerning the performance and resource consumption of the distributed BPEL executions still have to be considered, due to the fact that the distributed BPEL processes are executed on resource constrained devices which cannot operate as fast as back-end systems and might lack of resources during long-running lifetime. In future, we will try some real-time experiments to achieve sound comparisons regarding performance and resource consumption.

There is also another decentralizing approach using peer-to-peer WS Composition, which introduces more advantages than the distributed BPEL orchestration. However, it is still not widely accepted like BPEL and still lacks of support from the community. More effort will be put on the feasibility analysis of using WS-Choreography (2004) to implement this Peer-to-Peer Composition approach in the manufacturing domain.

In this paper, we mentioned the static approach of BPEL distribution, which means at the design time, the original BPEL process could be examined with partitioning rules and then partitioned and distributed to several locations at deployment time. More advanced optimizations would be the dynamic self-healing (automatic discovery and correction of failures) and self-optimization (automatic restructuring for optimization purposes) behaviours of the processes at runtime.

This work belongs to the SOCRADES project, aiming at the design and implementation of a comprehensive Smart Item Infrastructure for future manufacturing. Integration of SOA-ready devices into the enterprise domain must face the limitations of the dynamic nature of ubiquitous devices. More functionalities like dynamic service mapping and deployment, device and service monitoring, service discovery, etc should be supported by the integration. These issues can be tackled with the more capable middleware integration infrastructure (Moreira Sa de Souza et al. 2008).

## ACKNOWLEDGEMENT

The authors would like to thank the European Commission and the partners of the European IST FP6 project "Service-Oriented Cross-layer infRAstructure for Distributed smart Embedded devices" (SOCRADES - www.socrades.eu), for their support.

## REFERENCES

Baresi, L., Maurino, A., and Modafferi, S. (2006) "Towards Distributed BPEL Orchestrations" in *Electronic Communications of the EASST*.

Chafle, G.B, Chandra, S., Mann, V., and Nanda, V.G. (2004) "Decentralized Orchestration of Composite Web Services" in *Proceedings of the 13th International World Wide Web Conference*.

EU Project SiRENA (2005), online at http://www.sirena-itea.org/Sirena/Home.htm

EU Project SODA (2003), online at http://www.soda-itea.org/Home/default.html

EU Project SOCRADES (2008), online at http://www.socrades.eu/Home/default.html,

Fleisch, E. and Mattern F. (2005) "Das Internet der Dinge: Ubiquitous Computing und RFID in der Praxis: Visionen, Technologien, Anwendungen, Handlungsanleitungen", Springer Verlag.

Hackmann, G., Gill, C., and Roman, G.-C. (2007) "Extending BPEL for interoperable pervasive computing" in *Proceedings of the 2007 IEEE International Conference on Pervasive Services*, pages 204-213.

Hackmann, G., Haitjema, M., Gill, C., and Roman, G.-C. (2006) "Sliver: A BPEL Workow Process Execution Engine for Mobile Devices" in *Proceedings of 4th International Conference on Service Oriented Computing*, pages 503-508.

Jetty Web Server, Mortbay, http://www.mortbay.org/jetty-6/

kSOAP2 Sourceforge Project, http://ksoap2.sourceforge.net/

Mantell, K. (2005) "From UML to BPEL, Model Driven Architecture in a Web Service World", available online at http://www.ibm.com/developerworks/webservices/library/ws-uml2bpel/

Maurino, A. and Modafferi, S. (2005) "Partitioning rules for orchestrating mobile information systems" in *Personal Ubiquitous Comput.*, pages 291-300.

Moreira Sa de Souza, L., et al. (2008) "SOCRADES: A Web Service based Shop Floor Integration Infrastructure", in *Proceedings of the Internet of Things 2008 Conference*, Zurich, Switzerland.

Schlimmer, J., *et al*, (2006) "Devices Profile for Web Services" http://specs.xmlsoap.org/ws/2006/02/devprot/DevicesProfile.pdf

Sun™ Small Programmable Object Technology (SunSPOT) Theory of Operation (2007), Part No. 820-1248-10, Revision 1.0.8

WebSphere Everyplace Micro Environment (WEME), IBM product, http://www-306.ibm.com/software/wireless/weme/

Web Service Business Process Execution Language (WS-BPEL) version 2.0 (2007), OASIS standard, http://www.ibm.com/developerworks/library/specification/ws-bpel/

WS-Choreography (2004) http://www.w3.org/TR/ws-chor-model/

WS-Discovery (2005) http://schemas.xmlsoap.org/ws/2005/04/discovery/

WS-Eventing (2006) http://www.w3.org/Submission/WS-Eventing/

# TOWARDS OPTIMIZED MANUFACTURING SCHEDULING

Jing Chyuan, jing_chyuan@yahoo.com

School of Engineering Design and Technology, University of Bradford, Bradford, UK

## ABSTRACT:

*In this paper a novel approach is proposed to identify optimal solution of manufacturing system scheduling. Semi-Automatic Manufacturing System Scheduler (SAMSS) has been designed and developed to minimize total production time as well as total production cost. Genetic Algorithms, an optimization mathematical technique, will be applied to identify the optimal range for minimum and maximum cycle time of each workstation that produces different parts in the manufacturing system. Also simulation software, Arena, will be used to simulate and examine the manufacturing system that will be scheduled by the use of SAMSS. Finally, the results and future work are concluded in this paper.*

*Keywords: Genetic Algorithms, Simulation, Scheduling, Manufacturing*

## INTRODUCTION

A complex manufacturing system consists of multiple production lines that each line requires various resources such as steps and machines for completion. Hence the production engineer in manufacturing plant should manage resources in the optimal way. To meet on-time delivery and the objectives such as minimum product completion times, a reliable production schedule is essential. Nowadays, due to the increasingly competitive in global economies, scheduling has become very significant. Often the failure in addressing uncertainties such as a long queue time is the cause of unsuccessful scheduling. However, the scheduling problem can be effectively solved by the use of probabilistic model such as Genetic Algorithms (GA) to represent the uncertainties and preferences.

In this paper, a GA-based scheduler will be designed to solve the scheduling problem by finding out the optimal solution that minimizes the total production time and thus reduce the total production cost. First, we will introduce the concept of Genetic Algorithms and discuss the scheduling problems in manufacturing environment. Second, the methodology of scheduler is discussed. Third, the GA-based scheduler will then be tested and validated for reliability and accuracy in a simulation model in Arena. Fourth, the result and analysis are discussed. The research project is finally concluded with recommendation for further work.

## BACKGROUND

In engineering maintenance, construction, entertainment production, distribution, transportation, and manufacturing, scheduling is essential and plays a key role in the success or failure in a mission-critical activity. Scheduling is the process of setting times for activities in the plan, assigning resources, and choosing between alternative plans. Scheduling is also a process of optimization where overtime among both sequential and parallel activities are allocated by the limited resources.

Wall (1996) identified that a schedule requires fundamental data algorithms and structures, descriptions of performance measures and the objectives, explanation of relationships between resources and tasks and the models of processes that link them together. Scheduling requires a combination of varieties of data. At specific times, schedules allocate tasks to resources or resources to tasks. From machining operations, activities or tasks may be anything to software growth modules. Resources normally include raw material, human resources, and machines.

Furthermore, dynamic and incomplete data are the main causes of scheduling problems (Wall, 1996). In reality, most scheduling plans are subject to poor estimates, incomplete data, or unanticipated disturbances and hence it is not static. As a result, an optimal schedule has to be adaptable to constraints and the dynamic problem structure and at the same meeting existing constraints.

## Literature Review on Scheduling with Genetic Algorithms

The following discussion is about some case studies on the business and industrial sector scheduling with the use of Genetic Algorithms to solve scheduling problems and minimize total production time.

Chang *et al.* (2007) proposed Genetic Algorithms are able to solve the combinatorial optimization of nondeterministic polynomial-time hard (NP-hard) problems and also able to minimize the total completion time for the scheduling problems of no-wait flow shop. They show that to increase throughput, to reduce work-in-process inventory, and to minimize job average spent time in the production system are equivalent to minimizing the total completion time. They believed that the no-wait flow shop problem of zero setup time in the two-machine can be solved by developing an effective and efficient heuristic Genetic Algorithms. An initial population with a new crossover operator and simple heuristics is generated solutions for the problems. Also large sized NP-hard problem are solved by the Genetic Algorithms, but it is seldom to use in practice as it is being sensitive to Genetic Algorithms parameter and low convergence speed. Improvements have to be made for Genetic Algorithms in order to apply in reality.

Wang *et al.* (2005) proposed a Hybrid Genetic Algorithm (HGA) that is effectively used for minimize the completion time and for permutation flow shop scheduling with limited buffer. They identified that Local Search is enhanced by the Neighbourhood Structure and multiple Genetic operators are used to construct the HGA as the result for well balanced on the utilization and examination abilities. Based on benchmarks, the HGA effectiveness is demonstrated by the comparisons and simulation results. In addition, they divided the problem of scheduling into two types which are no-wait flow shop and blocking flow shop. Blocking flow shop problem is defined that the next machine is unavailable and cause the job remained at current machine. While the no-wait flow shop is defined as from the beginning to the end, every job must be processed smoothly either on or between machines. They believed that the utilization of Genetic Operator and Local Search are controlled by the use of a decision probability in order to concentrate computing effort and explore better solution space. In conclusion, they proved that the HGA used toughness and effectiveness solving the problem of scheduling with the utilization of the control and combination between Local Search and Genetic Operators.

Croce *et al.* (1995) identified Genetic Algorithms had been successfully used for the solving the job shop problem with total completion time criterion. He used Genetic Algorithms for scheduling in sequencing that allowed to reduce the waiting time as the total production time are also been minimized. Wall (1996) agrees that genetic algorithms as a solution method for the complex, combinatorial nature of most scheduling problems. Problems in which the objective and search space combine both separate and continuous variables were performed well by genetic algorithms. Genetic algorithms can be used for searching large, multi-modal spaces effectively because genetic algorithms run on a population of solutions rather than on one individual and apply other problem-specific information. Moon *et al.* (2005) identify that genetic algorithms are able to solve the problems of advanced planning in a manufacturing supply chain with a local search. They came out with a result showing that a more appropriate or suitable solution had been found by the genetic algorithms when the problem sizes were became bigger. They proposed the genetic algorithms can be effectively used to solve the complex and fairly large problem in a manufacturing supply chain.

Bertel and Billaut (2004) identified Genetic Algorithms as a means to solving scheduling problems where the problem is to carry out jobs between a due date and a release date in order to minimize the tardy jobs weighted number. They referred to a company that the transporters bring checks problem and considered the workshop is a flow shop of three-stage multiprocessor, with at some stages that allowed the job can re-enter in the particularity, and at each stages that allowed uniform parallel machines. This problem aspect can be called as Recirculation. They identified that the scheduling problem can refer to the eight jobs routing in the workshop which are packaging, sorting and printing, correction of data capture errors, manual data capture for non-scalable checks, data capture, capture of the identification number, scanning of checks, and preparation of lots. After the experiment with those scheduling problems, they proved that Genetic Algorithms can solve the difficult problems efficiently by going through with repeating Genetic Algorithms process of Generating Initial population, Crossover Operator and Mutation Operator. They proposed Genetic Algorithms as a decision maker for unexpected overwork cases to select the unimportance jobs to delay and important jobs to treat in priority.

**Summary of Researches**

Referring to the literature review, it can be concluded that most of the researchers are successfully using Genetic Algorithms to schedule or reschedule jobs sequences in which the jobs are given a due date to be completed in manufacturing system that minimized total production time as solved the scheduling problem such as bottleneck. Morton and Pentico (1993) also argued that schedule on the job sequences by finding the optimized job arrangement by using mathematical techniques such as Genetic Algorithms. Furthermore, Chang et al. (2007), Wang et al. (2005) mentioned that solve the Blocking Flow Shop Problem or bottleneck and provided No-wait Flow Shop in manufacturing system will provide fast and reliable production environment.

Hence, a novel approach of manufacturing system scheduling had been proposed in this paper to identify the best range for minimum and maximum cycle time of each workstation in the manufacturing system by using Genetic Algorithms. This approach is to minimize workstation average spent time based on its foundation as well as minimize the total production time.

## SEMI-AUTOMATIC MANUFACTURING SYSTEM SCHEDULER (SAMSS)

According to Goldberg (1989), the natural evolutionary process is simulated by Genetic Algorithms that can refer to any search process. There are possible solutions in solving a problem in a current population. In each generation, the parents mixing features occur on the best individual solutions to produce new population. On the other hand, the poor individual solutions are eliminated from the population in order to keep population stable.

Genetic Algorithms is an optimization technique that based on a population which is supported by a group of strings. Strings that had been represented as members in the population can be called as individuals or chromosome and they are evaluated by an objective function for select the optimal individuals to the next generation. In cycles, successive generations are generated by the random population which is initialized and gradually developed. In each generation, genetic operators and selection mechanisms affect the evolving population. Genetic operators include reproduction, crossover and mutation in which individuals provide information flow among them and the fittest individual survived the selection process. According to Goldberg (1989), by treating string chromosomes, Genetic Algorithms process schemata that are vast amounts of similarity templates, corresponding to numerous individuals not actually present in the current population. Through progressive recombination and selection, better strings are constructed from the best building blocks from past generations. Consequently, the evolution process moves toward the fittest individuals that allow the considered problem to be represented by near-optimal solutions. Goldberg (1989) argued that due to efficiency and low computational cost, Genetic Algorithms is applicable in search, optimization and machine learning.

The optimization of a system usually requires embedded analyses of the system in order to inform the optimization. These analyses are often in the form of a simulation. Kelton (1998) proposed that Arena is a simulation software which is easy to use and flexible due to its valid and quick decision making. Arena is also appropriate use for manufacturing systems that allow application of real systems behaviour to imitate by referring the general methods collection. As a result, there are many applications, industries, and fields that applied the idea of simulation across them. Simulation is used due to its ability to handle complicated systems by dealing with complicated models.

A GA-based scheduler, called as Semi-Automatic Manufacturing System Scheduler (SAMSS), will be designed, developed in MATLAB and tested in Arena simulation software. SAMSS is a scheduler designed to reschedule and minimize the total completion time on the manufacturing system. The main function of SAMSS is to find an optimal range for minimum and maximum cycle time between each workstation that allows the system to run with a minimum bottleneck hence minimizing the total completion time. Figure 1 illustrates the SAMSS interface and figure 2 shows all the operators and steps on SAMSS, and the explanation of the operators and functions are defined in the following discussion. SAMSS had combined six operators: Representative, Reproduction, Crossover, Mutation, Decimal to Binary Converter and Time Display.

SAMSS interface is for input three different kinds of data which are minimum and maximum cycle time for each workstation in the manufacturing system, number of population, and resolution number and it is able to create a new population that according to the input data. In addition, the input time is according to the system that needed to be scheduled, and the input data for population and resolution should be assumed by the user. Besides that, the buttons for others SAMSS operators had been created in the SAMSS interface as shown in Figure 1.

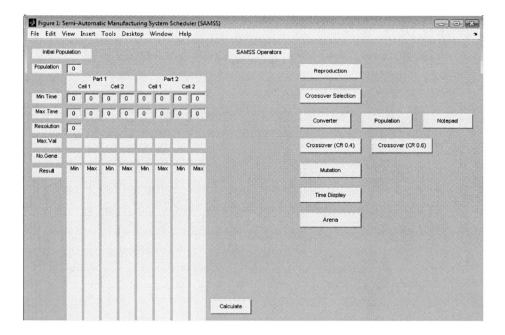

*Figure 1: SAMSS Interface*

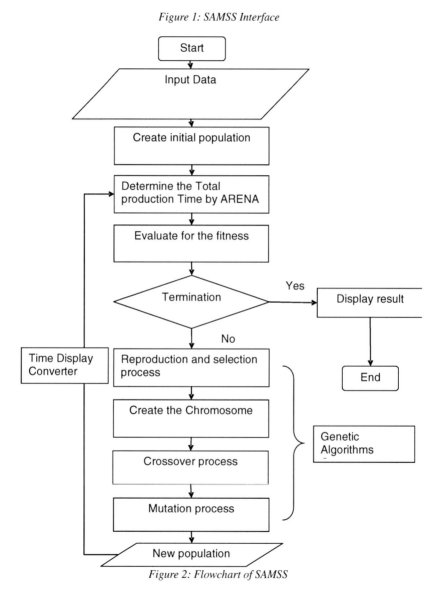

*Figure 2: Flowchart of SAMSS*

## Input Data

To allow SAMSS to create an initial population and an interface, the related information is required to enter into SAMSS. The information required are:

- Number of generation - SAMSS will stop process according to the number of generation that been given. It can be defined as a stop point for SAMSS.
- Number of population - The number of solution show in each generation. For example, the larger the number of the population input, the larger number of solution will be obtained.
- Fitness Function – The objective function for SAMSS.
- Crossover rate and Mutation – the rate for input into the crossover and mutation process.
- Number of parts to produce - The number of parts required to be produced in the manufacturing system, supplying information to SAMSS to create the interface.
- Number of cell (or workstation) -The number of cell in the manufacturing system that supply information in creating the interface of SAMSS
- The initial minimum and maximum cycle time for each cell - It allows SAMSS to search an optimal time for the cell due with the minimum and maximum cycle time that had been given.
- The production sequence of each part - SAMSS getting the optimal solution according to the part production sequence.

## Definition of Chromosome

In Genetic Algorithms, a chromosome can be called an individual. Chromosome is a set of binary numbers or parameters which describe an ideal solution to the problem that allow the Genetic Algorithms to be solved. The basic definition of chromosome is:

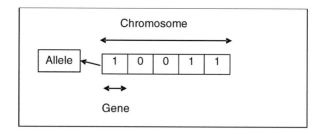

*Figure 3: Chromosome*

- Chromosome – a set of genes that are joined together
- Gene – a cell inside the chromosome
- Allele – one of two or more possible forms of a gene
- Locus – the position of the string
- Genotype – the combination of genes that a particular living thing carries
- Phenotype – the set of characteristics of a living thing (Goldberg, 1989)

## Definition of Fitness Function

Fitness function plays an important role in the Genetic Algorithms because the fitness function allows the quantification of the solution optimality which is also known as objective function. The relationship between the algorithm's goal and a perfect fitness function is closely connected, since the Genetic Algorithm might find the solution quickly due with the ideal function.

## Definition of Reproduction process

Reproduction can be explained as a selection process which is a process that individual strings from the initial population are selected and copied to the next population depending on their fitness function values. The individuals have a higher fitness values have a more chance to be selected and copied to construct next population. According to Goldberg (1989), roulette wheel selection generally is one of the common selection technique uses in reproduction process and it had been used in SAMSS.

Roulette selection begins with evaluating each current individual in the population through its fitness value. The total number needed to spin the weighted roulette wheel is due with the number of population and the reproduction candidate will presented (Goldberg, 1989).

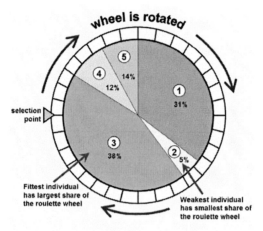

*Figure 4: Roulette Wheel Selections (John Dalton, 2007)*

From the Figure 4 that giving a summary that the individual from the initial population which have a higher fitness value have a higher number of offspring in the new population. The individual with a lower fitness value have a lesser chance to be selected to next generation. Besides the roulette wheel selection, there are other selections techniques such as stochastic universal sampling or Tournament selection which is frequently used in practice (Darrell Whitley, 2006).

## Definition of Crossover process

According to the Goldberg (1989), crossover is a process followed by the reproduction and selection process to construct a next population depending on the probability to pair the individuals and insert a new pair of individuals to a next population by exchanging the genes on the initial pair of individuals. If the crossover probability is high, the more number of individuals are paired. Sometimes a pair of individuals which had crossover will be exactly same as before. This happens because the crossover probability is low. Furthermore, the ways of exchanging the genes normally are using either one of uniform crossover, two point crossovers, or single point crossover. In this case, single point crossover had been used in SAMSS.

Single point crossover can be defined as the point to crossover is randomly chosen on a pair of individuals or a pair of parents. All data beyond that point is exchanged between the two individuals, the resulting individuals are called children as show in Figure 5

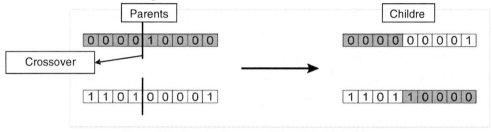

*Figure 5 Single point Crossover (Eiben & Smith, 2003)*

## Definition of Mutation Process

Mutation is a process followed by the crossover process to create a new population by changing the genes value in the individuals that had been randomly selected from the previous population (Goldberg, 1989). Mutation process is different than the crossover process which needs to select a pair of individuals. Mutation process only takes place on a single individual. However, the determination of mutation process is the same as crossover process which using the value of probability to run the process. In a set of individuals, each gene value is randomly created a variable is a common technique of implementing the mutation process. The change of the particular gene value is according to the random variable. The point of mutation is to avoid the similarity of the individuals between each other in the populations. Besides that, it also provides an opportunity to create a fittest individual in the next population by changing the individual's genes value randomly.

Mutation process in the binary individual can be defined as the gene value in the individual that is randomly selected in the binary individuals can be modified. The figure 6 shown an example that there were 3 individual's genes had been randomly selected from the particular individual and gene values are been changed from 0 to 1 or 1 to 0.

*Figure 6 Bitwise mutations for binary encodings (Eiben & Smith, 2003)*

## Definition of Termination process

According to Whitley (2006), termination process is one of the important processes in Genetic Algorithms because it terminates the continued generational process when it reaches the condition. The termination conditions are flexible and depend on the problem. Generally, termination's conditions are when it reaches the given generations number, or when it reached the top place solution's fitness, or when the minimum standard had been satisfied, inspection by manually or use the above condition together.

## Summary of this section

In this section, we have described the concept of SAMSS and the basic idea on developing SAMSS. Also SAMSS flowchart is to illustrate the operators and steps on SAMSS and the operations and functions are also explained.

Most of the operators and functions in SAMSS that are developed based on the Genetic Algorithm techniques. As a result, Genetic Algorithms is able to obtain the best fit values from each generation in an optimization approach. To prove that SAMSS is able to schedule the manufacturing system by identifying optimal range for minimum and maximum cycle time of workstations, a case study of small manufacturing system had been proposed and it will be discussed in the following section.

# IMPLEMENTATION

A small manufacturing system has been suggested by Kelton (1998). The layout of this system, shown in Figure 7, is made up of part arrivals, two manufacturing cells, and part departures. In the two manufacturing cells, each of them has one machine. The system is allowed to produce two parts and each is going through different sequence of the manufacturing cells.

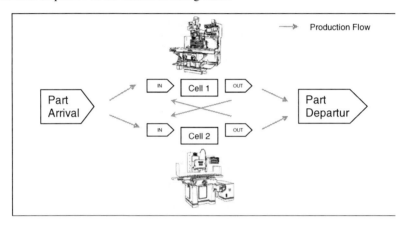

*Figure 7 Small Manufacturing System Layout*

A simulation model which shown as Figure 8 for the small manufacturing system is run by ARENA and it will give results of cells queue time and parts average cycle time. Therefore, SAMSS can study the average cycle time and evaluate optimal range for minimum and maximum cycle time by Genetic Algorithm techniques. After the time had been evaluated, SAMSS and the new range for minimum and maximum cycle time of cells will be input into Arena model to examine the time whether it has meet the requirement or not. If it did not meet the requirement, Genetic Algorithms will continue to evaluate and examine until it finds the optimal range time or reach the termination condition.

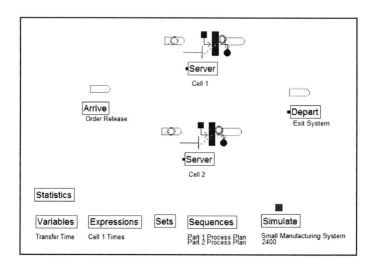

*Figure 8 ARENA model for Small manufacturing system*

## RESULTS AND ANALYSIS

In this paper, we discuss two results which are initial result and SAMSS optimal result. The initial result which evaluated by Arena that based on the original input data, while the SAMSS optimal result which evaluated by Arena that based on the optimal data and it determined according to the original input data.

The initial result and the SAMSS optimal result for the average total production time and average total idle time are shown in the Table 1

| Result | Average total completion time (minute) | Average total idle time (minute) |
|--------|----------------------------------------|----------------------------------|
| Initial | 55.628 | 34.088 |
| SAMSS | 35.171 | 13.869 |

*Table 1 Initial result and optimal SAMSS result*

As shown in Table 1, a big improvement is shown on the average total completion time and idle time between the initial result and the SAMSS result. There is a large time difference between the two results in which the difference of the average total completion time is 20.457 minutes and the difference of average total idle time is 20.219 minutes. This again proved that the relationship of average total completion time and average total idle time. Besides that, it can be argued that if the average total completion time is reduced around 20 minutes, the small manufacturing system will produce the part 1 and part 2 faster than the original system.

For example, if the manufactory produces the part 1 and part 2 in a week (1weeks × 5 working days × 8 hours × 60 minutes = 2400 minutes) and using the original manufacturing system, it will produce 43 parts (2400 minutes / 55.628 minutes each two parts = 43.144 parts). While using the optimum result which obtained by SAMSS, the manufacturing system will produce 68 parts (2400 minutes/ 35.171 minutes each two parts = 68.238 parts). As a result, it shown that by the use of the system which had been improved can produce more 25 parts in a week than the original system.

As a conclusion, it is proved that scheduling the manufacturing system with the use of SAMSS minimizes the total completion time and the total idle time. In addition, by minimizing the total idle time, the storage cost of the parts which are waiting to be produced or delivered can be reduced. Hence, SAMSS is able to improve and reschedule the manufacturing system for minimized total completion time as well as minimized total production cost.

## CONCLUSIONS

It can be concluded that Genetic Algorithms approaches can be used to develop schedule optimization algorithms. The test here was to minimize the total completion time, but the generality of the proposed approach means that any one or more selected process variables can be optimized simply by modifying the structure and definition of a chromosome. As a result, Genetic Algorithms is a suitable approach to solving manufacturing system scheduling problems, because they operate not only on a single solution but on a population of solutions. In scheduling the manufacturing system, it is shown that the population of solutions consists of many answers that may have different sometimes incompatible objectives. Hence, Genetic Algorithms is able to find the best compromise solution and obtain a set of non-dominated solutions with the large search space and small number of feasible solutions.

SAMSS can be a scheduling tool to implement Just-In-Time method in manufacturing systems. Just-In-Time method is defined as the production and supply of the required number of parts at the right time, which minimizes the inventory and eliminates the bottleneck. By the use of SAMSS to rescheduling manufacturing system, the time of jobs or parts that are waiting to be produced in the next workstation is reduced. Hence, the waiting parts warehouse and the bottleneck are also reduced and the production process flows more smoothly than the initial system. Hence, the production costs, such as the storage costs and delaying costs, are also reduced due to production increase.

# REFERENCES

Bertel, S. and Billaut ,J. -C., (2004). "A genetic algorithm for an industrial multiprocessor flow shop scheduling problem with recirculation". European Journal of Operational Research, Vol. 159, No. 3, pp. 651-662.

CHANG. Jun-lin, GONG. Dun-wei and MA. Xiao-ping, (2007). "A Heuristic Genetic Algorithm for No-Wait Flowshop Scheduling Problem". Journal of China University of Mining and Technology. Vol. 17, No. 4, pp. 582-586.

Cheung, Angus., Ip, W H., Lu, Dawei., and Lai, C L, (2003). "An Aircraft Service Scheduling Model using Genetic Algorithms". Journal of Manufacturing Technology Management, Vol.18, No.1, pp. 109-119.

Croce, Federico Della., Tadei, Roberto., and Volta, Giuseppe., (1995)." A genetic algorithm for the job shop problem". Computers & Operations Research, Vol. 22, No. 1, pp. 15-24.

Goldberg, David Edward, (1989). "Genetic Algorithms in Search, Optimization, and Machine Learning". Wokingham: Addison-Wesley.

H. Allaoui, S. Lamouri, A. Artiba and E. Aghezzaf, (2005). "Simultaneously scheduling n jobs and the preventive maintenance on the two-machine flow shop to minimize the Makespan". International Journal of Production Economics, Vol. 112, No.1, pp. 161-167.

Hadavi, Khosrow C., (1990). "ReDS: A Real Time Production Scheduling System from Conception to Practice. In: Monte Zweben and Mark S.Fox". Intelligent Scheduling. California: Morgan KauFmann. pp. 581 -605.

Hitomi, Katsundo., (1996). "Manufacturing Systems Engineering: A unified approach to manufacturing technology, production management, and industrial economics, Second Edition". London: Taylor and Francis.

Kelton, W. David, (1998). "Simulation with ARENA". New York: McGraw-Hill.

Morton, Thomas E. and Pentico, David W., (1993). "Heuristic Scheduling Systems with Applications to Production Systems and Project Management". New York: John Wiley and Sons.

Wall, Matthew Bartschi, (1996). "A Genetic Algorithm for Resource-Constrained Scheduling". Massachusetts Institute of Technology.

Wang, Ling., Zhang, Liang. And Zheng, Da-Zhong., (2005). "An effective hybrid genetic algorithm for flow shop scheduling with limited buffers". Computers and Operations Research, Vol. 33, No. 10, pp. 2960-2971.

Whitley, Darrell, (2006). "A Genetic Algorithm Tutorial". Fort Collins.

# AUTOMATED MARKET RESEARCH: CAPITALIZING ON THE FORESEEN CHANGES IN THE MARKET

Mark Isenbarger, Department of Information Systems and Operations Management, Miller College of Business, Ball State University, Muncie, Indiana, United States, mrisenbarger@bsu.edu

Jeff Davis, Department of Information Systems and Operations Management, Miller College of Business, Ball State University, Muncie, Indiana, United States, jtdavis4@bsu.edu

Brad Mier, Miller College of Business, Ball State University, Muncie, Indiana, United States, bdmier@bsu.edu

Department of Information Systems and Operations Management, Miller College of Business, Ball State University, Muncie, Indiana 47306

Supervisor: Dr. Fred Kitchens, Ball State University fkitchens@bsu.edu
(765)285-5305

## ABSTRACT

*The authors conducted rigorous research on the topics of digital signage, market research, Facial Recognition technology, and eye tracking technology to develop a solution to the marketing research challenge faced by their client, Enterprise Technology Group (ETG). The authors' followed the System Development Life Cycle (SDLC) to develop an appropriate and effective solution.*

*After the planning and information gathering phases of the SDLC, the authors determined that the optimal solution would be in house using off the shelf components. Three alternative solutions were contemplated: in-house development, purchasing an off-the–shelf solution, and contracting a third party. Once an alternative was identified, specific options were evaluated and reviewed.*

*The project was conducted during a two-semester senior course in Information Systems. The first semester was used for project planning, information gathering and analyze. The second semester was used for designing the new system, establishing contact with vendor, and developing an implementation and maintenance plan. The resulting solution is a first-of-its-kind, patentable process for measuring the consumer response to advertising on digital signs. The proposed solution was presented to ETG and was accepted. ETG will implement the project on all current and future digital signage instalments.*

*Keywords: Digital Signage, Redeye, Eye tracking, Facial Recognition, Systems Development Life Cycle*

# INTRODUCTION

Digital signage is one of the fastest growing marketing channels today. By 2011, it is expected to be a 3.5 billion ($ US) market. The leading companies in the digital signage market are NEC Display Solutions, Sony, LG, Samsung, Mitsubishi, Sharp, and 3M (Digital Signage Market Rapidly Expands, 2007).

The goal of advertising is to increase product awareness, increase sales, and to produce advertisements that have the maximum impact on the target audience, as measured by sales volume. Because it is difficult, if not impossible, to appeal to all potential customers, companies need market research in order to improve the content of advertisements. One of the purposes of market research is to study the target audience to determine the factors that contribute to the production of the best advertisement possible.

Digital signage is a form of advertising in which content such as messages, still photographs, and video clips can be displayed on an electronic screen, such as a flat screen monitor. Digital signage is widely displayed in locations such as restaurants, grocery stores, waiting rooms, pubs, airports, shopping centers, and banks.

Digital signage is a new technology in the field of marketing. Like most new technologies, it is still in the growth stage with much trial and error. Digital signs in waiting rooms are catching on, while digital signs at gas stations are failing. The giant American shopping chain, Wal-Mart, has found success in implementing digital signs in its stores, with 127 million people across the United States viewing the signs each week (Jones, 2007).

The purpose of this study is to develop a new application for the process of conducting market research process using digital signs.

## Profile of Client

Enterprise Technology Group (ETG) is an information technology (IT) company based in Indianapolis, Indiana in the Midwestern United States. It currently provides digital signage technology to multiple companies such as Buffalo Wild Wings restaurants, Kroger's Grocery stores, and Simon Properties Real Estate Offices. ETG's digital signage technology consists of flat screen monitors networked to a local computer. The local computer allows marketing content to be displayed at specific locations at specific times. ETG's digital signage is quickly replacing traditional advertising mediums, such as banners and posters for their clients.

## Profile of Student Team

The student consulting team is comprised of five students pursuing degrees in Information Systems, Operations Management, and Computer Science at Ball State University. The university is located in Muncie Indiana. Also known as by the nickname Middletown USA, Muncie has a rich history of market research because it is commonly considered a benchmark representation of American society. The university is within one hour and twenty minutes of ETG's headquarters in Indianapolis.

As a project for a two-semester course in Systems Analysis and Design, the student team acted as an independent consulting team working directly for Doug Sauer, President of ETG. The client approached the student consulting team with a project to develop a new application for digital signs in the field of market research.

## Challenge Statement

Digital signs are becoming a popular new method of delivering marketing messages and advertising products, promotions, and events. The purpose of digital signage is to deliver commercial messages that will result in viewers taking a desired action, such as purchasing a particular product. The information collected by market researchers allows advertisers to create the most effective advertisement in order to maximize revenues by motivating consumers to purchase the advertised product.

ETG anticipates digital signage, as an emerging marketing media, will result in a change in marketing research is conducted. ETG's goal is to lead the market in developing automated market research methods that measure consumer reaction to marketing content delivered through digital signage. ETG's challenge for the student consulting team is to develop a system that will use digital signage to automate the market research process.

# ANALYSIS

The student consulting team followed the traditional Systems Development Lifecycle (SDLC) approach to design an automated market research solution for the client (Palvia & Nosek, 1993). The standard SDLC was followed throughout the project, including planning, analysis, design, implementation, maintenance and feedback. The resulting solution is a first-of-its-kind, patentable process for measuring the consumer response to advertising on digital signs.

The student consulting team was organized and members were selected based on knowledge, skill, and ability that could be applied to the project. Team standards were developed along with a two-semester work breakdown schedule (WBS), and team-building exercises were conducted (Wysocki, Beck, & Crane, 2000). Work in the analysis phase began with of three interviews with the client and members of the client's staff; field research; seminars; literature review; technology review; feasibility analysis including organizational, technological, and economic analysis; and risk analysis. This research led to the development of system requirements, alternative generation, and making a decision as to the future direction of the project.

## System Requirements

The following research conducted in the research phase, five key system requirements were developed:

1.  Ease of Installation: The system components must be easy to install. Customers using the system may request multiple signs; employees from ETG must be able to install these signs in a timely manner.
2.  Durable: All system components must be durable. The components must be able to endure and withstand severe and unexpected conditions such as; extreme temperatures, being accidently turned off and on frequently, withstanding inexperienced or untrained users, etc. Durability also allows them to be easily moved and altered without damage.
3.  Maintainable: The to-be system must be easy to maintain. ETG employees must be able to make any changes or updates needed to the system, in a timely manner.
4.  Standardized: All components must meet the same standards. This will allow ETG employees to make changes to any components quickly.
5.  Centralized Control: The system must be able to control the marketing content and track consumer behavior individually, on every machine, from one central control location; regardless of the geographic distribution of the signs.

## Alternative Generation

Following a thorough analysis of the system requirements, three potential methods of solving the clients challenge were analyzed:

- In house design
- Off-the-shelf system
- Outsource the project

The decision-making procedure used to evaluate the possible alternative solutions was the Multiple Criterion Decision Analysis (MCDA) (Belton & Stewart, 2002).

Through primary research, secondary research, seminars, and interviews with the internationally-recognized Center for Media Design (CMD) at Ball State University, it became apparent that two types of technology, currently under development, would enable the automated tracking of consumer behavior as they visually interact with a digital sign.

*Facial Recognition* is a type of software application used to identify or authenticate a person from a digital or analog video or still image. The current state-of-the-art Facial Recognition program uses a combination of analytic and holistic methods to assess 15 facial features with regions of the eyes, nose, and the mouth (Yan & Lam, 1998). The software has demonstrated success in the identification of the faces at different perspective variations. Cameras used in the Facial Recognition process collect images from specified security cameras. The system then measures the nodal points on the face such as the distance between the eyes, the shape of the cheekbones, and other distinguishable features. These nodal points are then compared to the nodal points computed from a database of pictures to identify the individual (EPIC.org, 2006). Currently, this technology is being employed by many different businesses and branches of the US government in an attempt to improve security. The current Facial Recognition technology can only capture a few individuals in a very close proximity to the camera. However, Facial Recognition technology is improving as technology continues to develop. Facial Recognition technology could become a valuable tool to conduct market research.

The successful applications of Facial Recognition, which fall into the domain of biometrics, have recently received significant attention. This is especially true in the areas of Information Security (for example; application security database security, file encryption intranet security, Internet access, medical records) and Law Enforcement (for example; advanced video surveillance, control and surveillance, portal control, post event analysis, suspect tracking, investigation). Facial Recognition technology has also grown to include gender differentiation (Brunelli & Poggio, 1992).

Facial Recognition algorithms are a particularly good example of an opaque technology (Hansen, 2003). The Facial Recognition capability can be imbedded into existing Closed-Circuit Television (CCTV) networks, making its operation difficult to detect. Furthermore, it is passive in its operation; it requires no consent from its targets because it is a 'non-intrusive and contact-free process' (Woodward, Horn, Gatune, & Thomas, 2003). Two big issues resulting from the feasibility analysis are whether or not social norms will allow Facial

Recognition and whether or not the local law will consider it an invasion of privacy.

*Eye tracking technology* is a process to monitor a subject's eyeballs to determine eye movement (Jacob & Karn, 2003). There are two basic technologies; the current and most popular method uses coronary reflections to track the movement of the eyes (*Traditional Eye Tracking*). This technology has been used to research the effectiveness of warning labels, user-friendliness of Web pages, and assessment of visual equity. (Berman, Fischer, Kugan, & Richards, 1989) (Jacob, 1995) (Chandon, Wesley, Bradlow, & Young, 2006). The results from small-scale studies have proven to be accurate. This method of eye tracking is extremely labor-intensive and applies only to small sample sizes in a laboratory setting, in which the subject's eye movements are calibrated prior to the study.

The second eye tracking technology, commonly referred to as *Red Eye*, uses an infrared technology to reflect the light off of the subject's eyes retina, allowing the camera to identify a pair of eyes, determine the direction they are facing and measure the duration of the gaze. This can be used to determine how many consumers pass the digital sign, which of them look directly at the sign, and duration of their gaze.

Eye tracking does not require, nor record, the identity of the individuals being viewed. It tallies and monitors the direction of gaze for individual pair of eyes. Therefore, personal privacy issues will not be an issue when using Red Eye technology. Red Eye technology can capture a greater population at one time in a larger field of view than Facial Recognition or Traditional Eye Tracking.

## Decision Making

The Multiple Criterion Decision Analysis in conjunction with Pugh method (Ullman, 2006) was used to generate structured and quantifiable decisions between the three alternative technologies: Facial Recognition, Traditional Eye Tracking, and Red Eye technology. Six criteria were developed to order to evaluate the three alternative technologies:

- Availability

- Security
- User-friendliness
- Cost
- Reliability/Accuracy
- Resiliency
- Scalability

The client was asked to apply a numeric weight to each criterion reflecting the importance placed on it. Independently, without regard to the weights applied by the client, the consulting team rated each of the three technology options using the MCDA and Pugh method to calculate a score for each technology. The results are depicted in Table 1: Multiple Criterion Decision Analysis. The highest rated of the three technologies was considered the chosen solution. The rates determined for each technology on each criterion are as follows:

*Availability* refers to the client's ability to purchase or develop the solution in a timely manner. Facial Recognition software is available; however, the application of the system is not feasible to meet the client's requirements. Traditional Eye Tracking technology is readily available as a components off-the-shelf (COTS) application (Majaranta & Raiha, 2002). It would need to be integrated into the automated marketing network. Red Eye technology is available as a COTS application. It would also only need to be integrated into the automated marketing network. The technologies were rated as: Facial Recognition 3, Traditional Eye Tracking 10, Red Eye 10.

*Security* refers to necessary precautions taken to guard the new system against crime, attack, and sabotage. This also includes ensuring the anonymity of the images that will be captured on the cameras. Facial Recognition technology uses descriptive factors for facial identification (Li & Jain, 2005). The Facial Recognition process recognizes a particular individual's face from a database. While providing more information, this may raise key issues in the privacy sector. Traditional Eye Tracking technology studies track the eyes of the subject; they do not record or recognize personally identifiable features (Jacob, 1995). Traditional Eye Tracking is capable of providing more information about the objects at which the subject is looking than is required for this application. Red

Eye technology is capable of tracking the number of consumers that pass by the digital sign and the duration of each gaze; it does not record or recognize personally identifiable features. The technologies were rated as: Facial Recognition 4, Traditional Eye Tracking 7, Red Eye 7.

*User-friendliness* looks at how transparent the system is to the consumer. The system must be user-friendly so that consumers will not alter their behaviour and the research will gain accurate information about their behaviour. Because Facial Recognition requires no interaction with the consumer, it is a non-intrusive video monitoring of their behavior. Traditional Eye Tracking would require extensive calibration of the each subject's eye movement before it can be used and may require the consumer to wear a head device. Red Eye technology requires no recognition by the consumer. It is a non-intrusive eye monitoring method of tracking consumer behavior. The technologies were rated as: Facial Recognition 10, Traditional Eye Tracking 2, Red Eye 10.

*Cost* of implementation includes hardware, software, system implementation, use, and maintenance. The higher rating indicates lower cost (because lower cost is desirable). Facial Recognition will require a substantially greater cost than the other technologies because of the equipment and software required. (Cardinaux, 2006). Traditional Eye Tracking technology is available as a COTS device, which would be relatively easy to integrate, but the technology is more sophisticated and expensive then Red Eye technology (Andiel, Hentschke, Elle, & Fuchs, 2002). Red Eye technology is available COTS and is easily integrated into the system with little modification. Red Eye is the least inexpensive of the three technologies. (Katz, 1993) (Mulligan, 2002). The technologies were rated as: Facial Recognition 3, Traditional Eye Tracking 6, Red Eye 8.

*Reliability/Accuracy* refers to the overall capability of the system to provide and properly process the image data and the validity, of the data. The system must meet the client's confidence standards. This requires the system to process the data reliably. The available Facial Recognition software is highly reliable; however the client has requested a system that will operate at a distance of eight to ten meters. Facial Recognition works at two to three meters. With initial calibration, Traditional Eye Tracking technology will indicate the exact point and gaze route, which will indicate specific where the eyes are looking (Zhu & Ji, 2004). Red Eye technology has reliability and accuracy sufficient to the client. It tracks the number of gazes and their duration; however, it does not provide the level of accuracy that Traditional Eye Tracking would provide. The technologies were rated as: Facial Recognition 4, Traditional Eye Tracking 10, Red Eye 6.

*Resiliency* refers to the overall ability to recover from a system failure in a timely manner. This includes the ability to withstand adverse conditions such as high humidity and extreme temperatures. Facial Recognition technology will rely on the resiliency of the hardware components and custom software; the software can be customized and can be developed to the desired level of resiliency. Red Eye technology will rely on the resiliency of hardware and COTS software; the software is already available at a commercial standard. Resiliency of Traditional Eye Tracking technology will rely on hardware and software; however, the software needs more precision because it is designed for laboratory conditions. There may be more hardware components involved than the other technologies if the consumer is required to wear a headset device; with more components, there is the greater possibility of failure with Traditional Eye Tracking technology. The technologies were rated as: Facial Recognition 6, Traditional Eye Tracking 4, Red Eye 6.

*Scalability* refers to the overall capability to add new software features, hardware, and installations. The system is required to be highly scalable for the client's expected growth. Facial Recognition scalability has two components. First, the addition of client accounts through the database. Second, for each additional account, it will require additional hardware. Traditional Eye Tracking requires three components to scale up. First, additional client accounts through the database. Second, for each additional account it will require additional hardware, which is the expensive segment of upgrading. Third, the purchase of additional consumer eye tracking head devices. Red Eye technology scalability has two components. First, the addition of client accounts through the database. Second, for each additional account it will require additional hardware. The technologies were rated as: Facial Recognition 4, Traditional Eye Tracking 1, Red Eye 4.

Using the MCDA in conjunction with the Pugh method, the weights given by the client and the rates applied to each technology criterion, the resulting scores for each technology:

- Facial Recognition 285
- Traditional Eye Tracking 270
- Red Eye 405

Based on these scores Red Eye technology was the chosen technology (Belton & Stewart, 2002). This analysis is available in Table 1 Multiple Criterion Decision Analysis.

Table 1: Multiple Criterion Decision Analysis

| Decision Matrix | | | | | | | |
|---|---|---|---|---|---|---|---|
| | | Facial Recognition Software | | Eye Tracking Software | | Red Eye Software | |
| Criteria | ETG Wieght | Rating | Total | Rating | Total | Rating | Total |
| Availability | 10 | 3 | 30 | 10 | 100 | 10 | 100 |
| Security | 5 | 4 | 20 | 7 | 35 | 7 | 35 |
| User-Friendly | 15 | 10 | 150 | 2 | 30 | 10 | 150 |
| Cost | 5 | 3 | 15 | 6 | 30 | 8 | 40 |
| Reliability / Accuracy | 5 | 4 | 20 | 10 | 50 | 6 | 30 |
| Resiliency | 5 | 6 | 30 | 4 | 20 | 6 | 30 |
| Scalability | 5 | 4 | 20 | 1 | 5 | 4 | 20 |
| Weighted Average Score | | | 285 | | 270 | | 405* |

*The highest number means the best solution. The Cost rating is invers the rest of the ratings.

*Table 1: Multiple Criterion Decision Analysis*

# DESIGN

After determining Red Eye technology preferable to the other technologies, the student consulting team developed a unique solution to the clients challenge. In accordance with the system requirements developed in the system analysis phase, the resulting system has packaged installation that can be shipped to a location and easily setup, has an self contained durable components has COTS components that can be easily maintained in case of failure, has standardized equipment to simplify maintenance and repair, and is Internet-based to accommodate centralized control.

The new system has three primary components. The first of the three primary components is the in-store components used to capture the consumers' gaze. The second component is the central online database used to store the data captured on location. The third component is a corporate account control center where content displayed on every digital sign at the client's locations can be managed from a central corporate account control center.

Every customer location may have multiple units. Each unit will consist of one monitor, one infrared camera, and infrared illumination lights. The local network infrastructure will be client-based because of the variability and availability of Internet access and number of digital signs in place.

The second component of the system will be the central online database. The database will store data for all customers, for all of the customer's digital signs. The database will be stored within a datacenter with security and redundancy.

The third component is the corporate account control center. Each corporate account will have the ability to control the media content being displayed on each individual digital sign at each location in real time. This provides the ability for customers to conduct market research based on the effectiveness of particular media advertising content and the ability to change advertisements at any given time period. The controller may want to change the content being displayed on the digital sign in each of the stores based on conditions such as time of day, demographics, location within the store, and social events. ETG will develop custom software with two components, called Push software and Play software, collectively called Push and Play, to manage corporate account control center activities.

The new system is designed to operate in 3 sequential steps, each corresponding to the three system components depicted in Figure 1 System Design and Operation. Step one involves the following components: consumer eyes, digital signage, Red Eye, and a personal computer (PC). The Red Eye device is placed on the digital sign and plugged into the PC using a USB connection. The sign is plugged into the PC in order to display the content being advertised. The PC will run the software to play the digital media and conduct the analysis of the data gathered from the Red Eye.

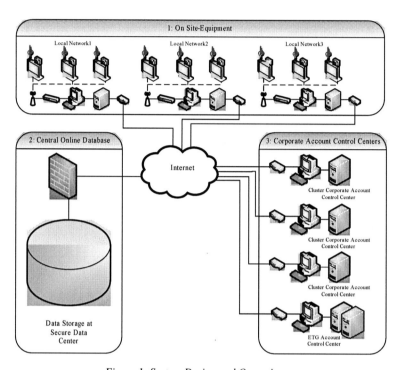

*Figure 1: System Design and Operation*

Once the marketing content has been uploaded by the PC, it is displayed through the monitor. As consumers walk by the monitor, the Red Eye device records the sets of eyes within in ten meters, records how many of those sets of eyes look at the monitor, and records the amount of time each set looked at the monitor. The data is collected by the Red Eye device and then processed by the PC using the analysis software. The data is then put into graphs and charts and sent out to the data center.

Step two involves the database and the information collected by each display. The data collected by each display will be sent to the online database. The clients can then log on under their account to see information relating to their advertisements. This information will be shown in charts and graphs generated by each location's PC. The database is hosted by the data center, and it is responsible for all of the maintenance.

ETG will provide Push and Play software for the corporate account controller to schedule media displayed on each of the digital signs in addition to retrieving the results from the database. Then, at the client's discretion, ETG will provide services to handle the client's corporate account center for a fee.

Step three involves the corporate account controller acting as the central controller and the advertisers. ETG will work with the advertising companies sending the advertisements to specific locations, determining what time the advertisements are going to be played, and deciding which advertisements need to be changed. This is where the advertisers will choose to send an advertisement to a specific sign or to specific stores. ETG, working as the central controller, can dictate which advertisements are being shown on each sign in each location across the entire network.

# IMPLEMENTATION

The fourth phase of the System Development Life Cycle is Implementation. In this phase an appropriate conversion style and location for the implementation of the new system. A hybrid direct conversion style, along with a pilot implementation was chosen.

## Conversion Style

A direct conversion style was chosen for this system. Some of ETG's current customers already have digital signs and may choose to upgrade to the new system. New clients will be shipped a complete system to be installed onsite. It is a complete switch from the old system to the new. ETG already has digital signage in the marketplace, but it does not have the automated market research system in place. Therefore, a direct conversion to the new system is the best choice.

## Conversion Location

A pilot conversion will be used to introduce the new system in a limited area on a trial basis. The existing customers who have chosen to upgrade to the new system will serve as the pilot location wherever possible. ETG will implement the pilot system on a few digital signage displays. This trial will ensure market acceptance before ETG offers the new system to new clients.

## Conversion Procedures

The conversion will be conducted in four phase:
- Phase 1: Install hardware
- Phase 2: Install software
- Phase 3: Network installation
- Phase 4: User training

There are two types of hardware installations that will need to be completed, depending on the client. ETG's existing clients already have digital signage displays. Therefore, they will need to add a Red Eye tracking device. Future clients will need to install both the digital signage display and the Red Eye tracking device.

ETG's Digital Signage Push and Play Software will be installed. Push software will be installed on each corporate account control center PC. The software allows a user on the control PC to schedule and "push" marketing content to each digital sign were it is played for the consumer to view. Play software will be installed onto the local PC controlling the digital signage.

The network at the client's location may be wired, wireless, and cellular depending on the number of signs purchased and the availability of the type Internet connection.

Clients at each corporate account control center will be trained on how to operate the system. Training will be provided by ETG and manuals provided by hardware and software vendors. ETG employees will be trained on how to install and operate the system. An employee at each digital sign location will be trained on use, maintenance, and minor repair issues.

## MAINTENENCE AND FEEDBACK

The maintenance will be handled initially by client's employees who are trained on the system at the time of implementation. If the customer's system cannot be fixed onsite, ETG will provide maintenance services. Upgrades and improvements will be provided by ETG, including new equipment as technical advances become available.

## PROJECT FOLLOW-UP

At the conclusion of the project, the results were presented by the student consulting team to the client, ETG, in April 2008 where they were accepted and approved. This was the conclusion of the consulting team's efforts on the project.  The client has subsequently met with the University's Director of Technology Transfer to work out Intellectual Property (IP) details and a licensing agreement in order to proceed with capital financing. The client has also met with the director of the local Business Incubator to discuss office space, business support, and local resources.  The client intends to move forward with plans to provide this service to future customers.

## CONCULSION AND FUTURE DEVELOPMENT

In addition to improving marketing effectiveness, automated market research has the potential to revolutionize the process of buying advertising space. Marketers would no longer buy space to advertise billboards or commercials at a particular setting but rather competing to outperform other organizations during specific times during day at specific locations. The advertisers are creating new content to sell their products in direct competition with other firms. With new information gathered from marketing research through digital sign, advertisers will be able to implement a more efficient pricing strategy. Marketing firms, manufactures, and retail outlets can better price their product due to near real time demand knowledge from their signs.

## ACKNOWLEDGEMENTS

The authors would like to recognize the professional collaborations of Ben Johnston, Fred Kitchens, and Brad Luetje. Additional appreciation is given to Ball State University, the Miller College of Business, and the Information Systems and Operations Management Department for supporting the System Analysis and Design sequence of course. Further credit is given to The Center for Media Design, Doug Sauer, and Enterprise Technology Group for their assistance.

## REFERENCES LIST

(2006, October 26). Retrieved May 25, 2008, from EPIC.org: http://www.epic.org/privacy/facerecognition.

Andiel, M., Hentschke, S., Elle, T., & Fuchs, E. (2002). Eye-Tracking for Autostereoscopic Displays using Web Cams. *Stereoscopic Displays and Applications XIII Vol. 4660* .

Belton, V., & Stewart, T. J. (2002). *Multiple Criterion Decision Analysis: An Integrated Approach.* Boston: Kluwer Academic Publishers.

Berman, E. J., Fischer, P. M., Kugan, D. M., & Richards, J. W. (1989). Recall and Eye Tracking Study of Adolescents Viewing Tobacco Adverstisements. *Department of Faimly Medicine* . Medical College of Georgia.

Brunelli, R., & Poggio, T. (1992). Hyperbf networks gender calssifiatoin. *In Proceedings of the DARPA Image Understanding Workshop*, (pp. 311-314).

Cardinaux, F. (2006). *FACE AUTHENTICATION BASED ON LOCAL FEATURES AND GENERATIVE MODELS IDIAP–RR 05-85.* Martigny – Switzerland: IDIAP Research Institute.

Chandon, P., Wesley, J. H., Bradlow, E., & Young, S. H. (2006, June). Measuring the Value of Point-of-Purchase Marketing with Commerical Eye-Traching Data.

*Digital Signage Market Rapidly Expands.* (n.d.). Retrieved June 17, 2008, from Digital Signage Resrouce.com: http://www.digitalsignageresource.com/digital-signage-articles/digital-signage-market-rapidly-expands.asp

Duchowski, A. T. (n.d.). A Breadth-First Survey of Eye Tracking Applications. *Department of Computer Science* . Clemson University.

Hansen, D. W. (2003). Committing Eye Tracking. *Ph.D. Thesis* . IT University of Copenhagen.

INSEAD Business School Research Paper No. 2007/22/MKT/ACGRD. (n.d.).

Jacob, R. J. (1995). Eye Tracking in Advanced Interface Design. *Human-Computer Interaction Lab* . Washington D.C.: Naval Research Lab.

Jacob, R. J., & Karn, K. S. (2003). Eye Tracking in Human-Computer Interaction and Usability Research: Ready to Deliver Promises.

Jones, B. (2007, March 8). *Wal-Mart takes in-store TV to the next level*. Retrieved June 29, 2008, from USA Today: http://www.usatoday.com/money/industries/retail/ 2007-03-28-walmarttv-tim-mcgraw_N.htm

Katz, W. J. (1993). *Patent No. 5270748*. United States.

Li, A. Z., & Jain, A. K. (2005). HandBook of Face Recognition.

Majaranta, P., & Raiha, K. J. (2002). Twenty Years of Eye Typing: Systems and Design Issues. *Symposium on ETRA 2002: Eye Tracking Research Applications Symposium* . New Orleans, Louisiana.

Mulligan, J. B. (2002, 7 2). Image Processing for Improved Eye Tracking Accuracy. NASA Ames Research Center.

Palvia, P., & Nosek, J. T. (1993). A field examnimation of systems life cycle techniques and methhodologies. In *Information and Management* (pp. 25 (2) 73-84).

Ullman, D. G. (2006). Making Robust Decisions: Decision Management for Technical, Business, and Service Teams. Victoria, British Columbia, Canada: Trafford Publishing.

Woodward, J., Horn, C., Gatune, J., & Thomas, A. (2003). Biometrics: A Look at Facial Recognition. *Documented Briefing prepared for the Virginia State Crime Commission* .

Wysocki, R. K., Beck, R., & Crane, D. B. *Effective Project Management*. 2000: Wiley Computer Publishing.

Yan, H., & Lam, K. M. (1998). An analytical-to-holistic approach for face recognition based on a single frontal view. *IEE Trans. Patt. Anal Mach. Intell. 20 (7)* , 673-686.

Zhu, Z., & Ji, Q. (2004). Eye and gaze tracking for interactive graphic display. *Department of Electrical, Computer and Systems Engineering, Rensselaer Polytechnic Institute* .

# MEDIA PRODUCTION AND EDITING: CAPITALIZING ON THE FORESEEN CHANGES IN THE MARKET

Nicole Smith, Department of Information Systems and Operations Management, Miller College of Business, Ball State University, Muncie, Indiana, nmsmith@bsu.edu

Supervisor: Dr. Fred Kitchens, Ball State University, Department of Information Systems and Operations Management, Miller College of Business, Ball State University, Muncie, Indiana 47306. fkitchens@bsu.edu (765)285-5305

## ABSTRACT

*Users posted more than 2,000 videos daily to the YouTube.com from May 15, 2008 to June 15, 2008 (YouTube, 2008). Advances in technology allow all computer users to create media content to post to the Internet. This includes amateur content filmed with a Web camera and professionally produced content posted on television and movie websites. ProduceNetTV is an Internet start-up company that will specialize in media production and editing, utilizing the Internet as a means of collecting and distributing its clients' media. This paper is an overview of a Systems Analysis and Design project to develop a cutting-edge solution to meet ProduceNetTV's vision of the future needs of its clients. The solution was developed following traditional Systems Development Life Cycle steps. ProduceNetTV accepted the design of the system in April 2008 and initiated implementation efforts in May 2008.*

*Keywords: Media Production, Media Editing, Internet Start-up, Emerging Media*

## INTRODUCTION

Users posted 64,200 videos to the Website from May 15, 2008 to June 15, 2008, and monthly viewers have increased from 20 million in 2006 to 70 million in 2008 (YouTube, 2008; MSNBC 2006; Sandoval, 2008). As online media content becomes more prevalent, demand grows for media production and editing services. The term "media" refers specifically to digitally generated audio or video content. ProduceNetTV recognized the need for Web-based production services for media content creators and requested a system design to allow the company to provide these services. The company will have two main activities: 1) receiving and producing live media content and 2) editing pre-recorded media. Both activities will be performed to the media content creators' specific requirements.

## Profile of Client

ProduceNetTV is an Internet start-up company that plans to enter the media production and editing industry by being the first company to provide media production services over the Internet. The company is based in Indianapolis, Indiana, United States of America. Its goal is to receive live and pre-recorded media from clients via the Internet. The primary contact from ProduceNetTV was Doug Sauer, Founder of ProduceNetTV. The company saw an opportunity to penetrate a new customer segment within the media production and editing industry by producing live media feeds and editing pre-recorded media over the Internet. The industry currently focuses on high-end clients; ProduceNetTV aims to appeal to smaller clients that are cost-sensitive by offering a high-quality product at a low price. In September 2007, ProduceNetTV requested a system design and technology strategy to enable live online media production and editing, which will be the cornerstone of the company's services and is not currently offered by any other company.

## Profile of Student Team

The student consulting team was comprised of five senior Information Systems students specializing in Systems Analysis and Design. To fulfill project requirements in a two-semester sequence of senior-level courses in Systems Analysis and Design, the students acted as an independent consulting team and worked directly with the founder of ProduceNetTV. The team designed a system to allow the company to penetrate an emerging customer base within the media production and editing industry by using the traditional Systems Development Life Cycle (SDLC) methodology (Avison and Fitzgerald, 1999).

## Challenge Statement

As professionals and amateurs continue to post new media content to the Internet each day, the need for media production and editing services has increased. Live broadcasts of news events and podcasts have become more prevalent, including the live Webcast of the CBS Evening News (Johnson, 2006). Currently, the editing market is designed for high-end clients that need editing of pre-recorded media. Large businesses and organizations can afford to spend money on these services, but they are often too costly for smaller businesses and amateur media content creators. Businesses in the media production and editing industry traditionally receive these files through the postal service or over the Internet. Clients that desired production services produced their own media content. ProduceNetTV requested a system design to satisfy the low-cost and high-quality needs of its potential customers and to lead the foreseen addition of Web-based production and editing services to the industry.

## ANALYSIS PHASE

Research was compiled on the business processes utilized in the media production and editing industry to supplement the requirements given by ProduceNetTV in the initial phase of the project. The client approved a set of criteria to evaluate three types of alternative approaches: an in-house solution, an outsourced solution, and an off-the-shelf solution. The client gave each criterion a numeric weight based on its importance to the company; the alternative approaches were ranked numerically on each criterion after performing research on each alternative's ability to satisfy the criteria. Multiple Criteria Decision Analysis (MCDA) was performed to determine the best solution for the company (Belton and Stewart, 2002; Dennis, Wixom, and Roth, 2006). After determining the most appropriate alternative approach and conducting further research, MCDA was performed on a set of specific alternatives and a second, more detailed set of criteria to determine the final solution and network design for ProduceNetTV.

## Primary Research

An initial meeting with Sauer and two of his staff members was conducted to research ProduceNetTV's goals for entering the media production and editing industry and the company's system requirements. Sauer outlined three main requirements for its system design:

**Requirement 1:**   The system will allow employees to produce live media content and stream it to media content providers.

**Requirement 2:**   The system design will facilitate remote production of live media and editing of pre-recorded media.

**Requirement 3:**   The system will provide space to store securely completed client media files.

Monthly status report meetings were held with Sauer to update ProduceNetTV on the project and review work completed during the previous month. During these meetings, the client discussed any changes related to the project, and follow-up questions were discussed. Sauer was contacted by telephone or email to answer any questions that arose between meetings.

## Alternative Approaches

Three alternative approaches to develop a solution for ProduceNetTV were evaluated:

- Approach 1: In-house solution
- Approach 2: Outsourced solution
- Approach 3: Off-the-shelf component solution

An *in-house solution* would allow ProduceNetTV to have control over the development of features and functionality of the solution, and it would allow continuous input from the producers and editors. ProduceNetTV employees would create the system. This solution is often used in situations where employees have the experience required to build the system (Dennis, Wixom, and Roth, 2006).

An *outsourced solution* would build upon the experience of an external design team (Dennis, Wixom, and Roth, 2006). ProduceNetTV would have input in the design process and control the product features. It will differentiate its product from competitors' products so it can create a competitive advantage (Porter, 1985). If the company uses an outside design team, it risks loss of information if the nondisclosure agreements are violated.

An *off-the-shelf component solution* is designed for an overall market or business process. Since this encompasses a broad variety of companies, uses, and industries, the product itself may not directly fit the needs of ProduceNetTV. The off-the-shelf component solution would allow ProduceNetTV to enter the market more quickly but would still require piecing together components or enhancing a single component (Dennis, Wixom, and Roth, 2006; CodeLance, 2007).

After extensive research on available solutions and comparing the options with the needs of the company, it was determined that the off-the-shelf solution was most appropriate for ProduceNetTV.

## Specific Alternatives

After determining the type of solution required by ProduceNetTV, the Pugh Method was used to perform Multiple Criteria Decision Analysis (MCDA) on the Specific Alternatives Matrix to quantifiably determine the solution that would best fit the needs of the company (Dennis, Wixom, and Roth, 2006; Krajewski, Ritzman, and Malhotra, 2007; Ullman, 2006; Belton and Stewart, 2002). Because ProduceNetTV is attempting to do something that has not been done previously, the solution will require either multiple components pieced together or a single component with significant enhancements. After speaking with people experienced in editing and producing media, conducting research on the product, and speaking with several technical support personnel for local technology companies about the possible solutions, more than ten possible approaches were narrowed down to the top five most viable alternatives. These five alternatives were included in a decision matrix to which MCDA was applied to quantifiably determine the most appropriate solution:

- Alternative 1: Adobe Premier Professional CS3 for editing with WebcamXP for production

- Alternative 2: Avid Liquid Chrome Xe for editing with WebcamXP for production
- Alternative 3: Pinnacle Studio Ultimate 11 for editing with WebcamXP for production
- Alternative 4: VT[5] for editing and production
- Alternative 5: Buyout of WebcamXP for editing and production

Each alternative contains a solution for media production and a solution for media editing; some alternatives, like Adobe Premier Professional CS3 with WebcamXP, require two packages to complete the editing and production processes.

*Adobe Premiere Professional CS3*, the editing component of Alternative 1, allows users to edit pre-recorded media. Many off-the-shelf programs provide this functionality, but Adobe allows users to create Blu-Ray discs. The program's controls are intuitive, which will decrease the training time. It supports a wide variety of formats and distributes media files to the Internet and mobile devices (Adobe Systems, Incorporated, 2008). However, users have complained of slow rendering speeds, which could drastically affect editing time (Stafford, 2007). WebcamXP, the production component of Alternatives 1, 2, and 3, is a small software-based solution for live production. The software was designed for inexperienced users. Producers can complete their work remotely on their own computers. WebcamXP also streams live media over the Internet. Some features used in production have been simplified to increase usability, which could create problems during production for ProduceNetTV because the features may not perform to the extent required by ProduceNetTV (Moonware Studios, WebcamXP home, 2008).

*Avid Liquid Chrome Xe* shares functionality with all professional-grade editing packages and is the editing solution for Alternative 2. The new release supports high definition formats and supports a variety of codecs (Pinnacle Systems, Liquid Chrome Xe, 2008). Avid has been used to edit movies and television shows such as "Lost" and "Heroes," and more than 75 nominees at the 2007 Emmy Awards used Avid to edit the media content (Avid Technology, Inc., 2008). The widespread use of the program suggests the quality and stability of its features, which makes it a viable editing package for ProduceNetTV. WebcamXP would be used for media production.

*Pinnacle Studio Ultimate 11* is a media editing software package and is the editing component for Alternative 3. Pinnacle Studio is comparable to other editing products and contains all core media editing tools that would allow ProduceNetTV editors to edit their customers' media. However, it is designed primarily for media capturing and high-definition formats (Pinnacle Systems, Inc., Pinnacle Studio Ultimate version 11, 2008). WebcamXP would be the solution for media production.

*VT[5]* is an integrated production suite developed by NewTek. It is a fully integrated solution for media editing and producing. Unlike the other alternatives, VT[5] is a computer system that contains a central processing unit, a monitor, a keyboard, a mouse, and a specialized iVGA card that allows the user to produce live video. The VT[5] system offers the functionality ProduceNetTV producers and editors require for either an editing or production project. Some of these functionalities include live switching, web streaming, real-time keying, titling, and the ability to produce a live show remotely (NewTek, Inc., VT[5] integrated production suite, 2008).

*WebcamXP's* producer, Moonware Studios, is a very small company with fewer than eight employees. Because the company is so small, ProduceNetTV should consider a buyout to restrict early competition by forcing other new entrants to create their own software solutions. It can perform production and editing fuctions, but its editing capabilities are limited. The software will be customized to the exact specifications of ProduceNetTV. Hiring the production staff of Moonware Studios would also be advantageous. ProduceNetTV would have dedicated programmers on staff to produce the best product for the company.

After meeting with ProduceNetTV about the specific alternatives, a second set of criteria was developed:

- Criterion 1: Support
- Criterion 2: Reliability
- Criterion 3: Cost
- Criterion 4: User-friendliness

- Criterion 5: Performance
- Criterion 6: Process complexity
- Criterion 7: Mobility

The client assigned numeric weights to each criterion based on its importance to the company. The criteria were weighted on a scale of 1 to 10; a weight of 1 is least important and 10 is most important. Each alternative received a numeric ranking based on its ability to satisfy the criteria. The criteria were ranked on a scale of 1 to 10; a rank of 1 means that the criterion has a low capacity to fulfill the client's need, while a grade of 10 means the criterion has a high capacity to meet the need. Using MCDA, the weight of each criterion and its ranking for each alternative were multiplied to obtain a rating of its effectiveness in meeting the needs of the client. The scores for each criterion were added to obtain a total rating for each alternative.

*Support* must be available to clear up any problems with the system because the live production process depends on a reliable system; a lack of support could cause ProduceNetTV to miss production opportunities. The two highest-scoring solutions are VT[5] and the buyout of WebcamXP. VT[5] support technicians can connect to the systems remotely and provide real-time, hands-on support. However, the support staff is not available after 5:30 p.m. each day (NewTek, Inc., Support, 2008). The buyout of WebcamXP would provide the most support because the program's creator would be onsite to fix any problems. In the support criterion, Adobe Premiere Professional CS3 with WebcamXP received a 4, Avid Liquid Chrome Xe with WebcamXP received a 5, Pinnacle Studio Ultimate 11 with Webcam XP received a 3, VT[5] received a 7, and the buyout of WebcamXP received a ranking of 8.

*Reliability* is crucial to ProduceNetTV's operations because of the importance of uptime in live production. Downtime could cause ProduceNetTV to miss valuable production opportunities. Alternatives 1, 2, and 4 have the highest ranks. Adobe Premiere Professional CS3 and Avid Liquid Chrome Xe are well tested in the mass market; both products experience high uptime (Stafford, 2007; Harvey, 2005). However, WebcamXP is untested in the commercial market, so it lowers the rank for the use of Alternatives 1 and 2. VT systems have been available to the mass market for several years, and NewTek has thoroughly tested the system (Mills, 2008). The specific solutions received the following rankings for the reliability criterion: Adobe Premiere Professional CS3 with WebcamXP ranked 7, Avid Liquid Chrome Xe with WebcamXP ranked 7, Pinnacle Studio Ultimate 11 with WebcamXP ranked 5, VT[5] ranked 8, and the buyout of WebcamXP ranked 6.

*Cost* is not the most important criterion because ProduceNetTV is concerned primarily with the functionality of the system. However, the cost must be reasonable for a start-up company. Ratings are based upon the total cost of the system, including the hardware required to run the solution. Alternatives 1, 2, and 3 are the most cost-effective solutions, but Alternative 3 was the least expensive overall. Pinnacle Studio Ultimate 11 with WebcamXP and a desktop system configured at Dell.com has a cost of approximately $858.94 (Pinnacle Studio, Inc., Pinnacle Studio Ultimate version 11, 2008; Moonware Studios, Order, 2008; Dell.com, 2008). The most expensive alternative is the buyout of WebcamXP. For the cost criterion, Adobe Premiere Professional CS3 with WebcamXP ranked 8, Avid Liquid Chrome Xe with WebcamXP ranked 8, Pinnacle Studio Ultimate 11 with WebcamXP ranked 9, VT[5] ranked 6, and the buyout of WebcamXP ranked 1.

*User-friendliness* is important because of the time constraints involved in becoming a first mover. ProduceNetTV can enter the market faster if producers and editors can learn the system quickly. This criterion includes the considerations of ease of use and training. Alternatives 3 and 5 have the highest rank. Pinnacle Studio Ultimate 11 is designed for the less experienced user, so it will be easier to learn. WebcamXP, which is included in the both alternatives, is also user-friendly; it was designed for home users. The solutions received the following rankings for the user-friendliness criterion: Adobe Premiere Professional CS3 with WebcamXP ranked 6, Avid Liquid Chrome Xe with WebcamXP ranked 5, Pinnacle Studio Ultimate 11 with Webcam XP ranked 7, VT[5] ranked 6, and the buyout of WebcamXP ranked 8.

The *performance* criterion has two components: production and editing. The client's weight of 10 was split equally between the two, and each was ranked separately. Production and editing are equally important aspects of ProduceNetTV's business. Production performance is important because any bugs in the system could cause ProduceNetTV to lose production jobs and clients. Editing performance is important because a large or complex editing job places strain on the program's ability to perform properly. For production, only two solutions could be used: WebcamXP and VT[5]. WebcamXP offers production ability, but it does not have as many features as VT[5]. In production, Adobe Premiere Professional CS3 with WebcamXP ranked 7, Avid Liquid Chrome Xe with WebcamXP ranked 7, Pinnacle Studio Ultimate 11 with WebcamXP ranked 7, VT[5] ranked 9, and the buyout of WebcamXP ranked 8. During the editing process, Adobe Premiere Professional CS3, Avid Liquid Chrome Xe, Pinnacle Studio Ultimate 11, VT[5], and WebcamXP could be used. In editing, Adobe Premiere Professional CS3 with WebcamXP ranked 8, Avid Liquid Chrome Xe with WebcamXP ranked 9, Pinnacle Studio Ultimate 11 with WebcamXP ranked 5, VT[5] ranked 9, and the buyout of WebcamXP ranked 5.

*Process complexity* can increase the time required to complete a project. To maximize profit potential, ProduceNetTV must have a quick turnaround time. WebcamXP is the least complex alternative because only one program is used for the editing and production processes, and it is user-friendly. The VT[5] system also has a high process complexity rating because only one system is involved in the editing and production processes. The five solutions received the following ranks for the process complexity criterion: Adobe Premiere Professional CS3 with WebcamXP ranked 4, Avid Liquid Chrome Xe with WebcamXP ranked 3, Pinnacle Studio Ultimate 11 with WebcamXP ranked 5, VT[5] ranked 8, and the buyout of WebcamXP ranked 9.

*Mobility* will allow ProduceNetTV employees to have the ability to edit and produce media from their homes or on the road. The ability to be mobile will allow ProduceNetTV to hire producers and editors from across the United States. Adobe Premiere Professional CS3, Avid Liquid Chrome Xe, Pinnacle Studio Ultimate 11, and WebcamXP are equally mobile because they can be installed on laptops. The VT[5] is slightly less mobile because users must connect to the device through the Internet to make the solution mobile. In the mobility criterion, Adobe Premiere Professional CS3 with WebcamXP ranked 9, Avid Liquid Chrome Xe with WebcamXP ranked 9, Pinnacle Studio Ultimate 11 ranked 9, VT[5] ranked 7, and the buyout of WebcamXP ranked 9.

The total score for each solution was calculated based on the weights and rankings. Pinnacle Studio Ultimate 11 with WebcamXP received 332, Avid Liquid Chrome Xe received 354, Adobe Premiere Professional with WebcamXP received 356, and the buyout of WebcamXP scored 400. The chosen solution, VT[5], scored 418. The results are shown in Table 1: *Specific Alternatives Matrix Using Multiple Criteria Decision Analysis.*

| Criteria | Weights | Alternative 1 Adobe with WebcamXP | Score | Alternative 2 Avid with WebcamXP | Score | Alternative 3 Pinnacle with WebcamXP | Score | Alternative 4 VT[5] | Score | Alternative 5 Buy WebcamXP | Score |
|---|---|---|---|---|---|---|---|---|---|---|---|
| Support | 9 | 4 | 36 | 5 | 45 | 3 | 27 | 7 | 63 | 8 | 72 |
| Reliability | 10 | 7 | 70 | 7 | 70 | 5 | 50 | 8 | 80 | 6 | 60 |
| Cost | 4 | 8 | 32 | 8 | 32 | 9 | 36 | 6 | 24 | 1 | 4 |
| User-Friendliness | 8 | 6 | 48 | 5 | 40 | 7 | 56 | 6 | 48 | 8 | 64 |
| Performance | | | | | | | | | | | |
| Production | 5 | 7 | 35 | 7 | 35 | 7 | 35 | 9 | 45 | 8 | 40 |
| Editing | 5 | 8 | 40 | 9 | 45 | 5 | 25 | 9 | 45 | 5 | 25 |
| Process Complexity | 8 | 4 | 32 | 3 | 24 | 5 | 40 | 8 | 64 | 9 | 72 |
| Mobility | 7 | 9 | 63 | 9 | 63 | 9 | 63 | 7 | 49 | 9 | 63 |
| **Totals** | | | 356 | | 354 | | 332 | | **418** | | 400 |

Table 1.  *Specific Alternatives Matrix Using Multiple Criteria Decision Analysis*

## DESIGN PHASE

After selecting the VT[5] system as the editing and production solution, a system was developed to meet the original three system requirements: 1) it allows ProduceNetTV to produce live media and edit pre-recorded media, 2) it allows its producers and editors to perform their job functions remotely, and 3) it provides storage for customer data. Extensive research was performed to determine what specifications were needed to perform media production and editing. To perform live streaming, ProduceNetTV must have one server with quad core AMD processors and at least 16 gigabytes of memory (Angel, 2008).

It should also have VMware installed to allow the server to handle Web server functionality. A Storage Area Network (SAN) will be used for scalable storage; it would also provide temporary storage for the Web and streaming server during maintenance.

To test the ability of traditional means of remote connection, including Microsoft Terminal Services Client and software-based Virtual Private Network (VPN) clients, test computers were set up; it was discovered that these means could not support the video connection and the response time for keyboard and mouse input was too slow to allow remote editing. Interviews with network administrators showed that hardware-based VPN appliances have frame rates high enough to support media editing (Angel, 2008).

The components of the system that will be housed by ProduceNetTV include: three desktop workstations; ten laptop workstations; a load balancer; two VPN appliances; a Web and streaming server; a SAN; a client data server; a domain controller; a firewall; three switches; ten KVM appliances; and ten VT[5] systems. Diagram 1: *Network Design* shows the internal infrastructure of the company and depicts how remote users access the system through the Internet.

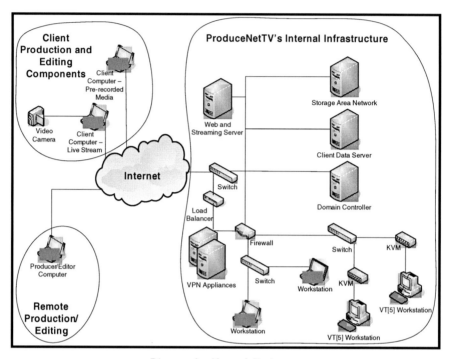

*Diagram 1.   Network Design*

After determining the system requirements, research was performed to determine which vendors had products that could perform to the product specifications required by ProduceNetTV. Dell is the recommended primary supplier for these components because it is the only manufacturer to offer quad-core AMD processors, which have more memory and more power than similar Intel chips (Fulton, 2008). To simplify product support, ProduceNetTV will purchase products from Dell whenever possible. Cisco will be the vendor for the VPN appliances because it was the only vendor capable of editing and producing video through its device.

Clients will send pre-recorded media and live streams over the Internet to the Web and streaming server. A switch connects the Web and streaming server, load balancer, and firewall to the Internet. Remote producers and editors can connect to the VT[5] workstations by connecting to the VPN appliances through the load balancer. They must go through the firewall and a KVM to connect to the VT[5] system. The KVM allows the producer or editor to use his or her own keyboard, monitor, and mouse to control the VT[5] without using the VT[5]'s resources. Internal desktops and laptops connect to the network through a switch and the firewall. Internal users will access the SAN, where completed media are stored; the domain controller; and client data server.

## Web and Streaming Server

One server will perform the Web server and streaming functions. This server must be powerful to handle all tasks it is assigned; these tasks include media streaming and the receipt of pre-recorded media files. To maximize the ability of system resources, VMware will be installed on the system. VMware utilizes the SAN to make task switching and machine maintenance simpler. The Dell PowerEdge 6950 was recommended based on technological capabilities at the time of the proposal.

## Domain Controller and Client Data Server

Both the domain controller and client data server require the services of unsophisticated servers; they do not need to be as powerful as the Web and streaming server. The domain controller is responsible for all requests to access network resources. The client data server will contain all client information, from contact information to detailed production and editing requests. Because of the lower performance requirements, the Dell PowerEdge 1950 III would be sufficient to perform the required activities based on technology at the time of the proposal.

## Storage Area Network

Storage area networks (SANs) cut the costs of storage and allow network administrators to upgrade servers easily. ProduceNetTV's SAN will hold all completed media projects and have space allocated to the Web and streaming server for upgrades. Because of the increasing need for storage as the business grows, a scalable SAN is very important. The Dell AX4-5 DEA was the recommendation at the time of the proposal.

## VPN Appliances

Virtual Private Network (VPN) appliances can connect to any network device, and users can access any workstation. ProduceNetTV must purchase VPN appliances that have enough bandwidth to allow producers and editors to edit and produce media remotely on the VT[5] machines. The Cisco ASA 5580-40 was the recommended VPN appliance solution at the time of the proposal.

## VT[5]

The VT[5] systems, by NewTek, allow ProduceNetTV to produce and edit media. These machines are the most essential element of the production and editing system. The VT[5] hardware runs on a Windows operating system, but the hardware is specialized to fit with NewTek's software. The ability to produce a live show is provided by the functionality of the iVGA connection, which allows the transfer of live media over an Ethernet connection. It also has push streaming, which allows users to stream live media to media content providers (NewTek, Inc., VT[5] integrated production suite, 2008).

## IMPLEMENTATION PHASE

Based on the system design, an implementation plan was created for ProduceNetTV. The plan has three phases: staffing; hardware implementation; and software and Website implementation.

### Staffing Phase

Based on expected demand for services, ProduceNetTV will initially hire 14 employees. The network administrator will maintain the network hardware and functionality. The Web administrator will maintain the Web server functionality and securing and updating the Website. The system administrator will ensure that the system functions properly and troubleshooting problems. The ten producers and editors will be responsible for working with the media. They will be hired before implementation of the hardware and software to ensure that the system functions the way they need it to function. The Web developer will create ProduceNetTV's Website. An outside contractor will fill this position and will be rehired to perform major upgrades on the Website as necessary.

## Hardware Implementation Phase

During the hardware implementation phase, ProduceNetTV will purchase and install the hardware required to run the system. The staff will be an integral part of system installation because they will maintain and upgrade the system in the future. A list of components was developed and presented to the client to detail the order in which components must be installed.

## Software and Website Implementation

After the hardware is installed, ProduceNetTV will install all software components. This includes configuring the servers, installing Microsoft Office, and securing the workstations with antivirus software. The Web developer will have a beta version of the Website running by this time to ensure that it functions properly.

# CONCLUSION

The completed 200-page system design, which detailed analysis, design, and implementation phases, was presented to ProduceNetTV in April 2008. The client, Doug Sauer, approved and accepted the proposal. The company is currently in the process of obtaining the capital funding required to implement the plan. ProduceNetTV has met with the University Director of Technology Transfer to discuss the intellectual property rights and has met with the Director of the local business incubator to discuss office space and local support.

# REFERENCES

Adobe Systems, Incorporated (2008), "Adobe Premiere Pro CS3" from: http://www.adobe.com/products/premiere/.

Angel, R. (28 February 2008), Personal Communication

Avid Technology, Inc. (2008), "Avid salutes the 2007 Emmy Award nominees and winners" from http://www.avid.com/emmys.asp.

Avison, D.E and G. Fitzgerald (1999), "Information systems development" in Rethinking Management Information Systems: An Interdisciplinary Perspective, Oxford University Press, Oxford, p. 250-278.

Belton, V. and T.J. Stewart (2002), "Multiple Criteria Decision Analysis," Kluwer Academic Publishers, Boston.

CodeLance (2007), "Custom software vs off-the-shelf products" from http://www.codelance.com/outsourcing-software-articles/custom-software-vs-off-the-shelf.shtml.

Dell.com (10 March 2008), "The Dell online store: Build your system" from http://configure.us.dell.com/dellstore/config.aspx? oc=ddcwfa1&c=us&l=en&s=dhs&cs=19&kc=productdetails~inspndt_530s.

Dennis, A., B.H. Wixom, and R.M. Roth (2006), "Systems Analysis & Design," John Wiley & Sons, Inc., Hoboken.

Fulton, S.M. (9 April 2008). "AMD quad-core Opteron servers claim performance records" from www.betanews.com/article/AMD_quadcore_Opteron_servers_claim_performance_records/1207780650.

Harvey, M. (2005), "Avid Liquid 7: A review by broadcast designer Mark Harvey" from http://library.creativecow.net/articles/harvey_mark/avid_liquid_7_review.php.

Johnson, P. (4 September 2006), "Evening news may have a reason to smile" from http://www.usatoday.com/life/television/news/2006-09-04-couric-main_x.htm.

Krajewski, L.J., L.P. Ritzman, and M.K. Malhotra (2007), "Decision making" in Operations Management: Processes and Value Chains, Pearson, Prentice Hall, Upper Saddle River, p. 25-43.

Mills, B. (1 April 2008), "NewTek VT[5]" from http://studiodaily.com/studiomonthly/currentissue/9257.html.

Moonware Studios (2008), "Order" from http://www.webcamxp.com/order.aspx.

Moonware Studios (2008), "WebcamXP home" from http://www.webcamxp.com/home.aspx.

MSNBC (10 October 2006), "Google Buys YouTube for $1.65 Billion" from http://www.msnbc.msn.com/id/15196982/.

NewTek, Inc. (2008), "Support" from http://www.newtek.com/faq/index.php?contact=tech.

NewTek, Inc. (2008), "VT[5] integrated production suite" from http://www.newtek.com/vt/.

Pinnacle Systems, Inc. (2008), "Liquid Chrome Xe" from http://www.pinnaclesys.com/PublicSite/us/Products/Consumer+Products/Advanced +Video/Liquid+Edition/Liquid+Chrome+Xe.htm.

Pinnacle Systems, Inc. (2008), "Pinnacle Studio Ultimate version 11" from http://www.pinnaclesys.com/PublicSite/us/Products? Consumter+Products/Home+Video/Studio+Family/Studio+Ultimate+11.htm.

Porter, M.E. (1985), "Competitive Advantage: Creating and Sustaining Superior Performance," Free Press, New York City.

Sandoval, G. (24 July 2008), "Sources: Google Video Soured Company on Long-Form Video" from http://news.cnet.com/8301-1023_3-9998420-93.html.

Stafford, A. (20 July 2007), "Adobe Premiere Pro CS3" from http://www.pcworld.com/article/id,134343/article.html.

Ullman, D.G. (2006), "Making Robust Decisions: Decision Management for Technical, Business, and Service Teams," Trafford Publishing, Victoria, British Columbia, Canada.

YouTube (15 June 2008), "Search" from http://www.youtube.com/results? uploaded=m&search_query=%2A.